WEATHER
ALMANAC

ERIC SLOANE

DOVER PUBLICATIONS, INC.
Mineola, New York

Bibliographical Note

This Dover edition, first published in 2013, is an unabridged republication in one volume of the following two books by Eric Sloane: *Eric Sloane's Almanac and Weather Forecaster,* originally published by Duell, Sloan and Pearce [and] Little, Brown, Boston, in 1955 and *Folklore of American Weather,* originally published by Duell, Sloan and Pearce, Boston, in 1963.

Library of Congress Cataloging-in-Publication Data

Sloane, Eric.
    [Almanac and weather forecaster]
    Weather almanac / Eric Sloane. — Dover ed.
       p. cm.
    "This Dover edition, first published in 2013, is an unabridged republication in one volume of the following two books by Eric Sloane: Eric Sloane's almanac and weather forecaster, originally published by Duell, Sloan and Pearce [and] Little, Brown, Boston, in 1955 and Folklore of American weather, originally published by Duell, Sloan and Pearce, Boston, in 1963"—Provided by publisher.
    ISBN-13: 978-0-486-49103-5
    ISBN-10: 0-486-49103-X
    1. Weather forecasting—Popular works. 2. Weather—Folklore. I. Sloane, Eric. Folklore of American weather. II. Title.

QC995.4.S56 2013
551.63—dc23

                                       2012051763

Manufactured in the United States by Courier Corporation
49103X01   2013
www.doverpublications.com

ERIC SLOANE'S

ALMANAC

and

WEATHER
FORECASTER

With 104 Illustrations by the Author

THIS FOREWORD is apart from my almanac: it is **A** my intention that you skip over it lightly, with the knowledge that it will be referred to many times later. **Foreword**

In doing this book, I tried to copy the format of old almanacs, because I believe that, like myself, most people enjoy the way weather data and rural observations can join together to make pleasant reading. **of Weather**

But the farmers and country people of the past, for whom the old almanacs were written, lived closer to nature and **Wisdom** were far more familiar with the anatomy of weather than we are today. Therefore, I think it in keeping to foreword my almanac with an abbreviated explanation of the mechanics of weather. As you later read the weekly accounts, you will find yourself constantly coming back to this outline and using it as a reference. Even more important, you will learn to use it in making your own weather predictions. Let's call it a miniature course in the anatomy of weather. The class, then, will please come to order!

A MINIATURE METEOROLOGY

Air. This film of stuff which clings to the earth (and in which we live) is an elastic, ever-changing material. It mixes and boils, expands and contracts; and it is swung into many patterns of movement by the spinning of the earth beneath it. Air inhales water from one place (evaporation) and spits it out in another place (precipitation); it lifts from the earth life-giving gases and plant seeds and moisture and salt and dust and countless other vital particles and moves them horizontally from place to place (wind). Although air is invisible, it is a real and ever-moving machine whose action enables life to exist within it.

If air ceased to move, there would be no weather changes. This idea sounds attractive to many. Perhaps it would be very nice, but then there would be no life on earth to appreciate it, for all living things are geared to weather changes.

Air Masses. Most people think that today is cooler because it is yesterday with some of its heat lost. Or they might presume that today is warmer because it is yesterday with heat added to it. Air, however, does not often stay still and just grow warmer or cooler. The air you exhale from your nostrils this second will be some five hundred miles away tomorrow; the air you inhaled was five hundred miles away from you yesterday. Weather, which is the condition of the atmosphere, is changed by new hunks of air which wander about the earth, pushed and pulled by the pressure machinery of sun heat. Fundamentally there can be only four differences between one air mass and another. It can be colder, warmer, wetter or drier. Naturally and normally, the colder air comes from the north, the warmer air from the south; the drier air comes from over dry land and the wetter air from over bodies of water. Of course there are combinations of these four qualities of air, such as warm-and-wet or dry-and-cold.

Fronts. As each parcel of new air approaches you to flow over and around you, there is first a collision between the air that you are in, and the front of the invading new mass. As soon as that collision has passed and you are then within the new mass of air, you will experience the settled change. The period of disturbance and collision is usually short— from ten minutes to ten hours—but the period of being within the mass itself is much longer.

DRAWING I

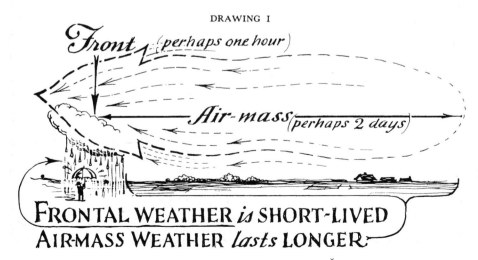

Front (perhaps one hour)

Air-mass (perhaps 2 days)

FRONTAL WEATHER *is* SHORT-LIVED
AIR-MASS WEATHER *lasts* LONGER

There are several kinds of fronts, but we can limit ourselves here to the cold front and the warm front. These, of course, are the bumperlike front portions of moving *cold* air masses or *warm* air masses, where they collide and where the disturbances of wind-shift, rain and storm occur. Cold air masses move faster than warm air masses and often catch up and overtake them, causing a whirlpool of rain and wind known as an occlusion. The faster the new air mass is moving and the greater difference there is in its temperature, the more storm fuss it kicks up when its front hits you. That is just like saying the faster an automobile goes and the heavier it is, the harder you get hit by it.

Sometimes there is very little difference between the present air mass and the new one that strikes us. Or the new one might have been moving very slowly. In either case, there might be no great "smashup," no noticeable storm or rain: the only way you could tell that a front had passed would be by a change in temperature, humidity and cloud-form. Drawing 2 shows that a cold front leans steeply backward and therefore gives less visible warning; a warm front leans gently forward and flows overhead with a warning parade of warm-front-type clouds. The dotted line in the drawing indicates the front.

DRAWING 2

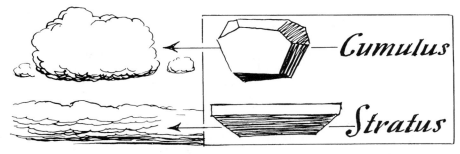

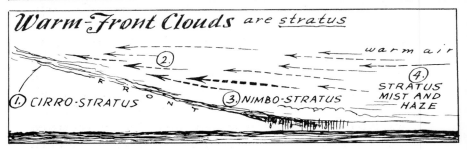

DRAWING 3

Clouds. Anatomically speaking there are only three kinds of clouds: CIRRUS, CUMULUS, and STRATUS. Outside of high-altitude wisps (CIRRUS), cumulus and stratus look like what their names sound like: accumulations (CUMULUS) and straight ceilings (STRATUS). Cold and warm fronts specialize in cloudforms of their own. You may often identify what kind of air mass you are in, or what kind of an air-mass front is approaching, by observing the clouds. Drawing 3 shows how the cold front specializes in lump clouds (cumulus types) while the warm front specializes in layer or "ceil-

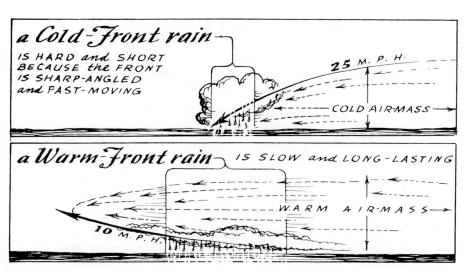

ing" clouds (stratus): this is usually true in both the storm front and the air mass behind it. The cross sections show the sequences of cloudform (1, 2, 3 and 4) as they appear. The cold front leaves dry, crisp air, high clouds and good visibility in its wake. The warm front leaves moist, warm air, lower clouds, and poor visibility. When the traveling air mass begins finally to wear itself out, its clouds start to look less typical. Drawing 4 shows the precipitation associated with both fronts. Warm-front rain lasts longer and is often more drizzly because its air mass moves slower and its front has a more slanting angle. Cold-front rain is usually shorter and more torrential because the cold air mass moves faster and the angle of its front is sharper.

Air Pressure. "Air pressure" is just another way of referring to air weight. The barometer measures the air's pressure by weighing it. In a mercurial barometer, the balance weight is mercury for no other reason than mercury's weight, its fluidity, and the fact that it will not evaporate. A mountain of air density above you will naturally weigh more heavily upon you than a valley of air density. The barometer, then, weighs the air above you and thereby ascertains if there is a "mountain" or a "valley" pressing down upon you. Drawing 5 shows how weather tends to flow off the mountains of density and to flow into the sink holes (low-pressure areas).

Air Movement. Moving air is called wind. Wind moves from high-pressure areas to low-pressure areas, but in a most indirect and seemingly strange manner. It first flows around the high-pressure area, all the while "leaning outward"; then it flows around the low-pressure area, all the while "leaning inward." This sounds confusing because words cannot adequately give you the picture, but the inset of Drawing 5 shows the phenomenon better. The steeper the slope of the atmospheric "hill" or atmospheric "valley,"

DRAWING 5

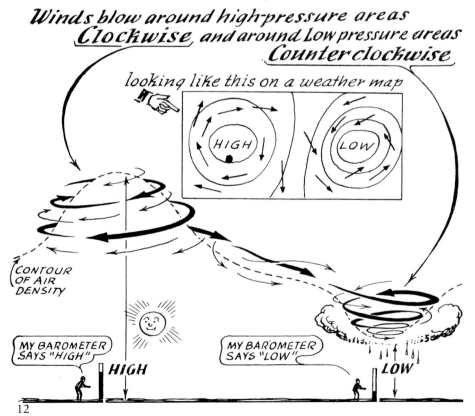

Winds blow around high-pressure areas Clockwise, and around Low pressure areas Counterclockwise

looking like this on a weather map

HIGH LOW

CONTOUR OF AIR DENSITY

MY BAROMETER SAYS "HIGH"   HIGH

MY BAROMETER SAYS "LOW"   LOW

the faster does the air flow downward (the higher is the wind). In the northern hemisphere the wind goes *clockwise around the high,* then flows *counterclockwise around the low.* (This rule is reversed in the southern hemisphere.)

The next two double pages show you the shapes of the clouds that will identify present weather and sometimes give you a clue as to what kind of weather will come tomorrow or the next day.

These are the Fair-weather Clouds...

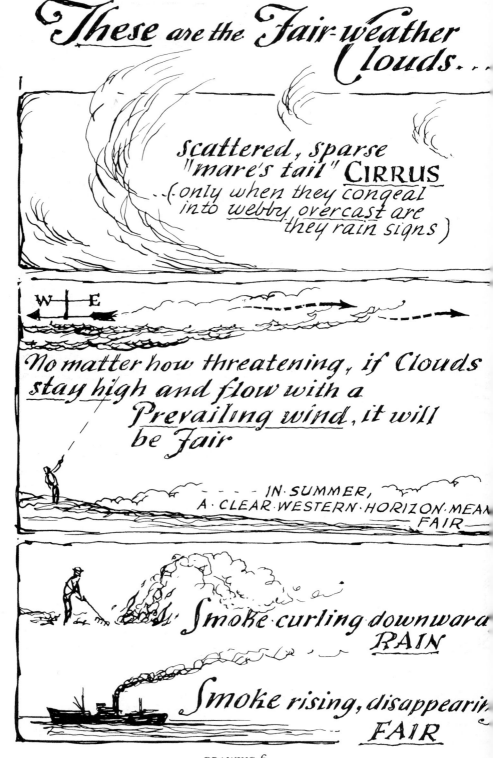

scattered, sparse "mare's tail" CIRRUS
...(only when they congeal into webby overcast are they rain signs)

W | E

No matter how threatening, if Clouds stay high and flow with a Prevailing wind, it will be Fair

IN·SUMMER, A·CLEAR·WESTERN·HORIZON·MEAN FAIR

Smoke curling downward RAIN

Smoke rising, disappearin FAIR

These are the Storm Clouds!

When Cumulus clouds become
TUFTED or CHAOTIC
(LIKE SHELLBURSTS)

Expect trouble!

HALOS·OCCUR·IN
CIRRO-STRATUS

a **Halo** AROUND·SUN·OR·MOON
FORETELLS·COMING·OF
The LONG·SLOW·RAIN·OF·A
Warm Front

(THIS·RULE·IS·TRUEST·in·SUMMER.)

Cirrus CHANGING·TO·WEBBY·OVERCAST·OF
Cirro-stratus

ENDS·IN·RAIN

USUALLY, THE·LONGER·THE·STORM
IN·COMING, THE·LONGER·IT·LASTS

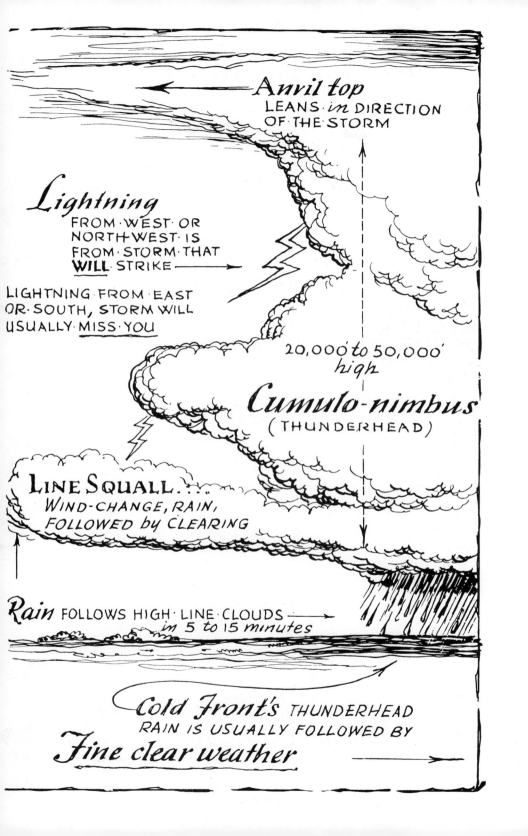

Anvil top LEANS *in* DIRECTION OF THE STORM

Lightning FROM·WEST·OR NORTH·WEST·IS FROM·STORM·THAT **WILL**·STRIKE

LIGHTNING·FROM·EAST OR·SOUTH, STORM WILL USUALLY·MISS·YOU

20,000' to 50,000' high

Cumulo-nimbus (THUNDERHEAD)

Line Squall.... WIND·CHANGE, RAIN, FOLLOWED by CLEARING

Rain FOLLOWS HIGH·LINE·CLOUDS *in 5 to 15 minutes*

Cold Front's THUNDERHEAD RAIN IS USUALLY FOLLOWED BY Fine clear weather

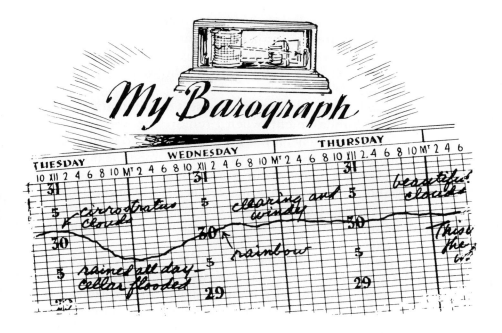

My Barograph

THIS BOOK was born on Christmas Eve. It was then, sitting by the fireside at Weather Hill, that I felt it suitable and satisfying to look back upon the past year. It struck me that the quick-passing moments and everyday observations of life in the country, those memories that we always go back to with such great pleasure, are easily lost in the routine of existence. That, I reflected, is why so many people keep diaries, which not only yield the satisfactions of a permanent record of one's activities but also evolve the greater enjoyment of bringing memories to life again. Like chopping your own firewood, which thereby warms you twice, doing things in this life is only half the joy; the other half and the more lasting pleasure is in remembering.

My barograph is the nearest thing to a diary in my life. The barograph, a weather instrument that is run by the

Author's Note

works of an eight-day clock, is a barometer which records atmospheric pressure on a chart that is marked with the days and hours of one full week. At the end of each week the barograph gives you a record of the weather pressure for the past seven days.

In itself, then, a barograph is a sort of automatic diary. But each Sunday night, when I remove the weekly chart and insert a new one, it has been my custom to write a few comments about the past week's weather upon the inviting, unused white spaces of the graph. Sometimes I have remarkable rainbows to describe, or the effect of dryness upon the vegetation. I might make notes on the amount of rainfall or whatever phenomena of weather that seem worthy of note.

It never occurred to me that in doing this I was keeping a diary until, on Christmas Eve, when going over the old barograph charts to refresh my memory of the past year, I found my penciled notes more revealing and more entertaining than the actual graphs. My immediate resolution for the New Year was to start out on January first with fuller comments on the weekly weather story, and to add whatever rural observations seemed pertinent, using all the white space on the back of each chart. I would include notes on research around the countryside and on the interesting things I learned each week.

Here in the countryside of Connecticut there is every chance to observe the open sky, to watch the cloud changes from day to day and from hour to hour, and to feel the effects of the weather and seasons upon the land and growing things. Perhaps such a weekly record as I could keep in this way would give pleasure to others too, especially to those who love the country but who, for one reason or another, are unable to witness nature's blessings as they appear on the earth's face and in the skies.

There are, in general, two kinds of people who are interested in weather. One is the scientist who watches and studies the phenomena of atmosphere with the purpose of forecasting weather. The other is the philosopher; he cares not if tomorrow brings rain or sunshine. He beholds the heavens and finds inspiration there rather than scientific prophesies.

The countryman is both scientist and philosopher. Weather is part of his working equipment and the sky is equally a backdrop for his pleasures. There are times when the weather is called "bad": that is when it interferes with us. As for myself, I have come to believe that the changeableness of weather is such a necessary fact of life's process that it is more often a pleasure than a nuisance. It is a constant challenge, fascinating in its infinite, unpredictable variety. So if the weatherman himself can be right only seventy-five per cent of the time, the rest of us might as well become weather philosophers and so learn to enjoy that remaining twenty-five per cent.

You can become your own weather forecaster, but it takes time and patience and observation. Above all, you must take regular observations and write them down. Your comments on a sky will have no special value or meaning or interest until they are connected with your observations about the weather that has followed. After a while you will begin to see that your every comment on the sky turns into a prediction.

Forecasting the future is no key to contentment, but to make the most of the moment at hand is a great art. Of two men looking at a sunset, the scientist will say, "Tomorrow will be clear," while the philosopher observes, "What a wonderful sunset!"

Eric Sloane

Weather Hill
Brookfield, Connecticut

an Early ICE-FISHING *house*

A LIGHT, HALF CLOUDY DAY. Very much, I think, like the heads of last night's partymakers. It is good to live in the country, where a deep breath of air seems so much more reviving and stimulating. The wind is from the east. If you "taste" it fully, you will recognize the tang of salt, fresh from the Atlantic.

A fine day for a walk to the lake, which I took with some anticipation, for I had been hoping that the uncertain weather had not melted the ice. But it was there, without a puddle of water to be seen. Some hardy individuals were out fishing through the ice: January is the month for catching pickerel and perch. From the shore, I spotted six fishers, each one spaced far apart, looking very lonely and still on the vast expanse of ice. They seemed to be wearing bright sweaters and caps; I fancy they were testing out Christmas gifts.

As a child I remember seeing ice fishers, but they fished from within little wooden shelters that were built exactly like country outhouses, outfitted with a bench and a kerosene heater. The whole contraption was sledded out to location either on runners that were a part of the shelter or on Junior's sled. I remember hearing my family tell about a country minister who would read the Bible while ice fishing and even prepared his sermons there. At that time, I wondered why a person would choose so strange a place to read or work, but now that the years have filled my ears with the confusion of everyday life, I can better understand the value of quiet. The people who used to fish through the ice seemed to be members of some sort of clan who enjoyed something secret from all others, they took their unexciting sport so seriously. Whether they caught a fish or not seemed beside the point; their day on the ice in seclusion and quiet always brought adequate satisfaction.

This day, like the notion that all Mondays are gloomy, is true to form with typically uncertain New Year's Day weather. But dark as they are, as long as the clouds are high and do not tend to lower, precipitation will not fall from them. It is not that high clouds do not produce rain or snow, but that rain or snow will evaporate back into the atmosphere before it reaches the earth when the journey down is such a long one. I remember flying among fair-weather cumulus clouds during fine days, yet getting a windshieldful of raindrops each time I passed beneath them. Another thousand feet below, the air would be perfectly dry.

When I first moved to Weather Hill and began remodeling the farmhouse, I had great hopes of finding ancient treasures hidden around the place. But although the house was built in 1782, the oldest piece of printed matter to be found was an 1818 *Farmer's Almanac* that had been tacked over a hole in the storeroom wall. I think it appropriate now to read from the first page of this book, titled "New Year's Day"; it tells in its own way how the people must have lived when this house was young. Oddly enough, the weather prediction for that day, over one and a half centuries ago, was exactly what today's weather is—"cloudy and uncertain." Some things change so little!

"Good morning," starts the first page, "it is good to see my friends. And you, my good friend, let me once more take a cordial shake by the fist. I am happy to see you in good spirits at the opening of a new year. Your barn, your sheds, your stables, your corn house, your wood house, your smoke house and all your possessions denote good husbandry.

"Now who is there so doltish as not to take pleasure and high satisfaction in viewing the bountiful productions of a well cultivated farm? a neat tidy house; a right and comfortable barn and stables; a wood house filled with seasoned wood; a plenty of hay and fodder; cattle bright and trim; a cellar full of sauce; tubs full of meat; garners full of grain; butter and cheese in abundance; the garret full of wool and flax; parlor and kitchen full of pleasant looks and soft words!" Amen to those days and to those thoughts.

Such words might give the impression that the early New Englander was a hoarder. But in those days, wealth was not measured in cash. Rather was it measured in a person's ability to make use of what nature provided and the manner in which he stored up against the stark days. Most things around a farm were traded, so there was little need for cash. Bank accounts were rare; one's entire wealth was usually invested in the farm. A farmer did not raise more than he needed for his own use, and his only cash crop was the standing timber that he sold when he cleared his woodlands.

The uncertain weather has lengthened the icicles around on the house; some of them are now over six feet long. I felt that they were a colorful part of the rural scene, even nursed them along until a neighbor explained to me that icicles on a house are a sign of lost heat. The melting of snow on a roof, it seems, is largely because of heat leaking through the attic. Those six-foot icicles, I later realized, probably cost me about ten dollars apiece, each one representing poorly insulated roofing.

It is interesting to notice how a house with no heat in it will hold snow and ice on its roof. As I look out now over the snow-covered hills, I can easily spot the barns with animals inside and those that are empty just by observing the snow or lack of snow on their roofs.

I went up to look at my own abandoned barn one night, curious to see if it had icicles. It hadn't. As I walked out into the night air, the snow complaining under my feet, I could easily imagine what it was like on such a night, over a century ago, when the barn was in use. I stood for a moment in the clear night air, imagining myself as the farmer going out to put the stock to bed. His candle lantern must have thrown grotesque shadows around these very same rocks. Inside the barn were once the warm living smells of animals and the musty tang of hay and manure. As I stood looking into the past, almost hearing the cows and restless clucking of hens in the barn, I forgot about my icicle research. The barn was silent and empty, stark as the night. This is the barn I shall take down as soon as the weather permits; it is weak, swayed by years of abandonment.

I felt sad as I followed the shaft of living-room light that flowed from the house and out over the patches of snow, certainly not the way that farmer of the past ever felt on

The Barn

his way back to his house. Just before I reached the kitchen door, a shower of fireplace embers rose silently from the chimney, and I awoke from my dreaming, and looked forward to the comfort and cheer of my living room.

Later, as I sat before the big fireplace, I promised myself that very little of the old barn's wood would find its way to this hearth. I'd save every bit of it I could, and make it a part of the house that the barn once belonged to, possibly as wall paneling or partitions. And where the barn stood, I shall plant a kitchen garden. I think the first owner of the place would agree with that. A good thought to go to bed with.

Stone-boat or farm-sledge

iron runners →

Second Week of January

"NOW MOVE YOUR STONES AND TIMBERS," reads the *Christian Almanack* of 1824 for this week; "transport your grain and salt and plaster on the first ice." This passage refers to a practice that few farmers consider now—the art of sledding heavy loads over ice. In the early days, wheels were used only for light loads; runners were used for all heavy loads. Where wheels would sink into the soft ground of yesterday's roads, sled runners on ice made the heaviest loads seem lighter. So upon the first freeze, and before the deep snow arrived, the collected heavy chores of farm work were done, with the oxen pulling large stones, loads of wood or other heavy material on a sled. In the early days, no one would have thought of moving heavy stones during summer. They were unearthed and rolled onto two logs, ready for sliding to their destined location as soon as winter and sledding time arrived.

Some sleds had no runners, such as one that I found in my barn: it was more properly called a sledge or stoneboat and was used primarily for moving large stones. The front steps of Weather Hill consist of two massive flat stones, ten feet long, that must weigh a ton apiece. I believe they were moved by this same sledge in the barn.

The unseasonable weather was broken this week by a cold wave from the northwest. There was no precipitation along the front of this new air mass, but the drop in temperature and the sudden change of sky, with high, small and very white cumulus cloud puffs, identified it as a purge of polar air. Tonight is very still and cold. Yet there are noises outside that seem to increase the coldness. From the oak grove on the hill, there is a faint but persistent snapping of twigs whenever the breeze stirs, and it sounds like the tinkling of a glass of ice water. Throughout the night there is the dull booming of ice in the lake as it freezes and expands, sounding like distant thunder.

An airplane pilot told me that he once saw such a crack at the instant it occurred. As he flew low over a frozen lake, his attention was directed to a narrow opening in the ice directly beneath his plane. As he watched, a crack shot out in an irregular manner, hurtling down the length of the lake at meteorlike speed. Then above the din of his airplane motor, he heard a thunderlike crack and boom, in his words, "like the snap of a whip."

It is good to feel the cold of winter, particularly when you were beginning to lose faith in the regularity of the seasons. The few days of good ice on the lake are more than I have seen anywhere for many years. Today there are ten-year-old children in New England who have never used a sled. Currier and Ives prints show the Hudson River as being the scene of great iceboat races, and there was a regular sled service at one time in New York between Manhattan Island and Staten Island. The Hudson River has not been frozen over for years but this year I think it will be.

It is interesting to note that the ice in the lake is noisiest when the barometer is up. I do not know whether it is the added weight of air pressure pushing the ice down, or that the coldness of high-pressure weather causes faster freezing. Perhaps it is both.

I get much pleasure from reading through my collection of ancient almanacs before going to bed. Particularly in an old house, it is an ideal way to end the day; there is always some choice piece of information that makes dozing off to sleep easier. My last night's reading enlightened me on the name of nearby Candlewood Lake. I had always regarded it as a name dreamed up by some real-estate developer. The almanac, however, gives a description of the proper way to prepare "candlewood." Candlewood was seasoned pine, cut into long slivers and used as torches before the days of kerosene lamps. Later, I learned much more at the New Milford Library, for it has records of Candlewood Mountain as being the ancient source of virgin-pine candlewood. New Milford merchants once sold both candlewood and pine knots for illumination, and nearby Brookfield supplied traveling peddlers with them.

I now recall an iron cage, open at the top and hung on a swivel, among the refuse that I foolishly gave to the junkman when I cleaned out the barns. I had no idea what it was. But the library showed me a picture of the very same thing, as hung in Boston for street lights before 1700. The cage held burning pine knots and it was kept fed throughout the night by the town crier. It was America's first street lamp!

You may scoff at talk about the old days being more romantic, but just as a dinner with candlelight is different from one lit by electricity, the nights of long ago were richer for their poor illumination. One of my finest childhood recollections is of the summer nights when I went down to the dock to fish for catfish. The blackness of the lake, the lap of water against the shore, and the cavernous darkness inside the boathouse made night exciting. And I recall later when we had electricity cabled to the island and lights installed along the dock. One flip of a switch robbed the night of its mystery and blasted that whole wonderful setting forever.

This morning while I was shoveling a path through some snow patches, I found many tunnels next to the earth. I had been wondering what happens to mice and other small animals in high snow, but they seem to get around very well underneath it! Judging by the variety in sizes of tunnel diameters, there were several species of animals: the whole maze was as complicated as the subway levels at Forty-second Street and Broadway. I've heard how animals will tunnel under the snow and feed all winter on the lower bark of trees, without once coming to the surface.

Mice are particularly destructive to small trees during the winter by attacking them from beneath the snow. This is called "girdling"; the result is sure death to the tree. The red man's word for girdling meant "tree choking." Copying this habit of rabbits and deer, the Indians girdled whole forest groves so that sunlight could reach their woodland garden patches. How odd that just from removing a thin strip of bark from around a huge tree and cutting into the cortex, it will die.

Almost every day during the past week I have seen sun halos in the sky. During summer this would have definitely

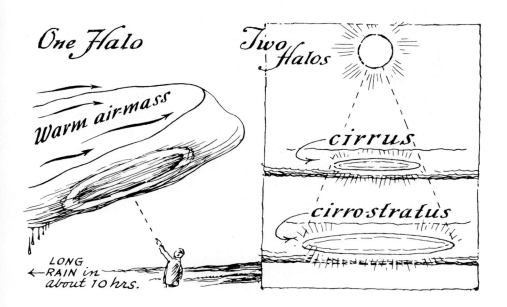

One Halo

Warm air-mass

LONG RAIN in about 10 hrs.

Two Halos

cirrus

cirro-stratus

indicated the approach of a warm front and rain. But in winter, the sky is so much colder that ice clouds occur lower and more frequently, so halos that occur when the winter sun shines through cirroform ice clouds have less rain-predicting significance than those of summer. Sometimes there are two or more halos when the sun or moon shines through two or more levels of clouds.

Over twenty-five thousand feet up, the season is constantly winter; the only difference is that the average "winter level" moves up or down about a thousand feet according to the time of year. Winter skies are lowest, summer skies highest. From there on up, all cloudform is composed of tiny ice crystals, which sound heavy and not at all like the sort of thing you'd think a cloud should be made of. But when you think that much of our ordinary "house dust" is of meteoric origin, you can understand how even iron may "float in the atmosphere."

Folklore is full of halo proverbs: "The bigger the ring, the nearer the wet," "The moon with a circle brings water in her beak," and, as the Zuni Indians put it, "When the sun is in his house, it will rain soon."

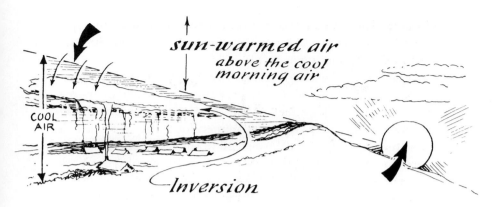

sun-warmed air
*above the cool
morning air*

COOL
AIR

Inversion

THE COLD AIR MASS has finally worn itself out and left an atmosphere of dull uncertain weather. Wherever sunshine reaches, there are thawing and mud.

I rose early this morning with expectations of ice skating, but my hopes dwindled as I found the path to the shore muddy and wet. Sure enough, the ice on the lake was melting.

On my way back, I stopped on the hilltop to look down toward New Milford, nestled in the valley. The town was hidden by haze and the smoke of many morning fires. The smoke could be seen to rise about a hundred feet and then level off into a stratus layer, looking more like fog than smoke. This effect of "inversion," as the meteorologists call it, lasts only until the sun has risen high enough to start atmospheric circulation going again.

The term *inversion* implies a reversal of the usual rule of air getting cooler with height. This rule aids the normal rise of smoke and the creation of clouds. But in early morning, when it is yet behind the horizon, the sun's first rays strike high-altitude air, warming it. So for a brief while during sunrise, you will find sun-warmed air aloft and dark, cold air below. The drawing shows that as the sun rises, the air that it has warmed aloft lowers and pushes down all air currents and smoke that would otherwise con-

Third Week of January

tinue to rise. You will see the same effect at sundown, when the lingering smoke of some campfire will rise and then level off to a foglike ceiling.

When I was a small child, my family had a summer house on an island. Every winter that lake froze over to a depth of about four feet of ice, and the commercial ice-houses on the lake were of tremendous size. The area's wealthier people, I recall, were all in the ice business. There were no electric refrigerators then, and much of New York and the surrounding cities were supplied with the lake's natural ice. The icehouses seemed large enough to fly air-planes in. During certain weather changes when the ice supply was low, clouds formed within these great buildings and actual rain and snow fell. Natural ice is becoming one of America's lost and forgotten industrial scenes: the horses and ice saws, the strange clan of ice cutters who worked only during the winter, were a part of American life that has never been pictured or written about. Now that many of the lakes don't freeze, those days seem even more remote.

We seem to have been in a period of weakening winters, caused by the melting of the polar icecap. The oceans have risen close to an inch in the past two hundred years and if the receding of polar ice continues, the experts say, the oceans in time will rise over a hundred feet and cover most of the large cities in the world. But cycles end, and in a few years we shall probably see iceboating on the Hudson, and New England children will get their sledding season back.

The morning paper has an article in it entitled, "Is the atomic bomb causing our mild winter?" I know the answer to that one—"No." As big a thing as an explosion can be, the air masses that cause weather are always infinitely big-ger. A moving warm or cold air mass may take in half the whole continent and would be very little affected by the largest atomic explosion.

The barometer is lowering and the night is moist and hazy. I hear much dog-barking in the woods and along the valley floor. Although the moon is ghostly tonight, and it is a perfect time for dogs to "bark at the moon," you can tell by their sounds that they have cornered some sort of animal. It is strange how many ways a dog may bark to make his message known. By listening to my dog I can easily tell whether he is barking at another dog, or a man, or if he has treed an animal. There is a special bark for a friend and another one for a stranger. There is one for food, a bark to enter the house, and another to go out. Yet all these messages are conveyed by one bark, different only in tone and expression.

The farmers here say that dogs are more capable of scenting a trail before a storm and I can understand why. Before a rain, when the air pressure lowers, many odors that had been held captive by the high pressure of good weather are released. You therefore might think that a hunting dog would do his best before a storm, but no. The sudden release of week-old scents will smell like fresh scents and thereby fool a dog.

It is well known that swamps and wet places smell more just before a rain. Decaying matter will often form gas that becomes imprisoned under mud in tiny bubbles. Lowering pressure bursts these bubbles and the gas flows out. "When ditch and pond offend the nose," goes an old saying, "look for rain and stormy blows."

Tonight the moon looks very old and tired as it floats in an uncertain heaven of cloud shreds. It is in its last quarter. The state of the moon has always been of first importance in almanacs, and during the early days of New England, the moon governed almost as many farm activities as did the sun. In January, during the moon's last quarter, most farmers were upcountry getting sawlogs out of the woods: "wood cut during the old moon of January and February" made timbers that stood straight and true. A farmer who cut his timber during the new or full moon could expect strange things to happen when it warped and split in his barn framework. Felled trees were also hewed into four-sided beams for house framework during the old moon, usually in March or May. The scientist does not acknowledge this custom to be anything but superstition, but the coldness of the air, the dormant state of trees, and possibly the midwinter state of tree sap, seem to have been important in the old-time seasoning of wood. Superstition or not, the lumber cut by plain farmers of yesterday cannot be equaled by the experts today. Weather Hill has half-inch pine boards twenty-six inches wide that are straight and without a crack after almost two centuries of weathering.

The word "seasoning" now means the proper drying of wood. But at one time it referred to the proper season of the year for felling and hewing. The drying of wood, so ancient books tell us, is more properly accomplished when it is worked upon during the right "moon" or "season of the month."

When apple blossoms bloom at night
For fifteen days, no rain in sight.
Old farm saying

36

I found several beautiful pine boards in the farmhouse pantry, some over twenty-eight inches wide, being used as shelving. These I removed and put in the kitchen as paneling, replacing them with two narrower pine boards from the local lumber yard. The dealer assured me that they were "kiln-dried" but as soon as they were placed in the warmth of my kitchen, they warped into such shapes that dishes slide off them. How interesting that what with all our modern machinery and scientific knowledge, we cannot do with wood what the ordinary farmer of yesterday seemed capable of.

Trees are so reactive to weather changes, it seems we might look to them for much weatherlore. Indeed, our most accurate way of learning past weather is to analyze the rings in the grain of ancient trees. We know by California's redwoods exactly what the weather was a thousand years before America was discovered. It seems possible that trees might also predict future weather.

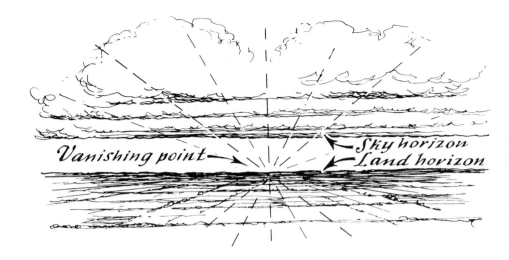

Vanishing point → ← *Sky horizon*
← *Land horizon*

Last Week of January

WINTER is a good time for cloud study. Clouds are lower then, and you may more easily study the perspective of the sky. Clouds are not "hung on a vertical wall at the end of the horizon" like a scenic set, but rather are placed horizontally along the "ceiling" of sky that extends from the far distance to directly overhead. There is always an obvious horizon of land, but when there is nothing to obstruct your view, you may also see the reversed horizon of clouds, as shown in the above sketch. The nearer cloud banks are to the horizon, the closer together are the horizontal lines of cloud bottoms, following the same pattern as landscape perspective.

When the countryside is covered with the white of snow, the color of the sky is especially evident. I have often wondered why so few people study the sky, particularly the artists who paint it. Museums of art contain more square feet of sky in their paintings than of anything else; yet no art school has bothered to teach their students how to paint it. There are special courses in painting animals, birds, trees, and almost everything you can think of, but nothing about the sky. The most talented artists often seem unaware of sky anatomy.

In landscapes, distance is denoted by shades of blue: distant mountains are bluer. But with clouds and sky, this rule reverses. Distant clouds are redder; nearby clouds are bluer. Thunderheads that hover on the horizon are always seen through a concentration of dust; like the setting sun, they are tinged with red.

This week has been more like winter. It started by a snowfall during the night, with just enough to cover the brown bare spots of earth. I recall closing up the house that night and thinking that I "sniffed snow in the air." I wonder what it is that enables us sometimes to sense snow or rain while it is yet on its way. It is probably a combination of many things—a change in humidity, air pressure, and all the subtle qualities of atmosphere that we take for granted.

One storm sign that I always enjoy observing is the hollowness of sound that occurs before a rain, as if distant outdoor noises are heard down a long corridor. I have never heard this discussed scientifically, but I do believe it is caused by a lowering of the atmospheric "sounding board." Whereas sounds ordinarily dissipate into space, the lowering of clouds and the change of air currents that accompany rain seem to throw back a special echo to distant sounds, making them seem nearer. One of my almanacs puts it nicely, saying, "Sound travelling far and wide, a stormy day will betide." The drone of a plane, the loudness of distant trains and the toot of a whistle are definitely different before a rain.

In the country, I find there are many prestorm sounds. One is the murmur of the forest without apparent wind. "When the forest murmurs, and the mountain roars, then close your windows and shut your doors," or, as Elijah said as he looked into the mountains, "There is a sound of abundance of rain." Not until I'd moved into these hills did I figure out a reason for this. All weather, it seems, starts from aloft and lowers to the earth: a change in wind or a beginning of wind always strikes the upper levels first and lowers to the earth as the storm approaches. The hills here are so towering and easy to observe that this rule of weather becomes quite apparent to me. The effect of hilltops blowing while trees close at hand are still is that of a supernatural sound of storm issuing from a quiet forest.

After the snowfall, there was a fine collection of snow on every tree branch, giving an impression of lace in the woods. This only happens with powdered snow, and when the snow falls in completely quiet air. It lasts until there is a stirring of morning wind, which dislodges the snow so the effect seldom lasts for more than a few hours, and occurs only a few times during a winter.

I used to think that snowfall was a silent action of weather but since living in the country, I have been more aware of the noise that snow makes as it falls, a sort of soft hiss.

When it is very cold and the snowflakes are crisp, there is a metallic tinkle, probably the tiniest of sounds.

I had asked Jimmy the farmer to come by today and help me turn over the blocks of granite and marble that form the patio outside my dining room. I lifted one of them when I came to Weather Hill and found it to be a tombstone, beautifully engraved with dates and a Biblical phrase. So I have decided to turn them all over and enjoy their fine lettering and ancient design. But Jimmy stopped by and said the snow and cold would make a poor time to do the job. "If you move them now," he said, "the frost will heave them." He further said that he didn't like fussing with other people's property, especially when they were dead. Previously he tried to discourage my gravestone patio by telling me it was unhealthy to sit outside to eat and drink. "Folks used to eat inside and go to the bathroom outside," he said. "Now they eat outside and go to the bathroom inside." I shall wait till after the frost to do the job.

I understand that the wavy and rickety condition of many old houses is due entirely to frost upheaval. Barns, which usually lie directly on ground stone foundations, often have roofs that have changed lines with the moving contours of the earth. Some of the barns with roof-lines that look like ocean waves are as firm as when they were built. If you look at the ground below, you will find that the earth has acquired the same lines.

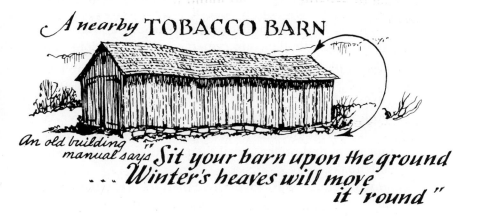

A nearby TOBACCO BARN

An old building manual says "*Sit your barn upon the ground ... Winter's heaves will move it 'round*"

West sunset sky . . . . . . east sunset sky too!

First Week of February

I THINK I shall like the old farm more and more. One of my worries about it was the fact that it does not face the west. When I mentioned this to friends and they asked me what difference that made, I told them that I enjoy watching the sun set. But since living here, I have made the discovery that the sun "sets" in the east also. What I refer to, of course, is not the sun itself but the sunset sky. We so often watch the setting sun and fail to look in the opposite direction. There, in the dull-lit eastern half of the sky, where the most dramatic changes occur, the lighting is indirect and the colors are more positive.

February second is Groundhog Day. I need not explain the legend; everyone knows it. I dislike repeating folklore that is stupid and without scientific reason. Such are the sayings that ridicule the countryman's weather wisdom and confuse the person who is genuinely interested in weather-lore. I have never heard of these animals coming out from hibernation before the end of March or the first of April so I cannot explain the early date of Groundhog Day. As fat and flabby as these little fellows are, I have much respect for them and prefer to call them by their proper name —woodchucks.

The woodchuck was originally called *wejack,* which was the early settler's pronunciation of an Indian word meaning "ground dog." Woodchuck meat is as tender and salty as chicken, and it is one of the few foods that a person lost in the woods without a weapon can catch. The woodchuck has great curiosity and he is slow to retreat. If you can find him away from his hole in the ground, and if you thrust your shirtsleeve down (with the cuff tied), the woodchuck can be chased into the den, sleeve and all.

In moving to the country, one always has an eye out for interesting people, those who have grown up with the land. Earl Gann, whom I have hired to work around the place, is such a person. Although he left this area as a young man to be a lumberjack and has returned with a Scottish accent after forty years, he still remembers much of the history of my house and of the farms nearby. The children around here call him "Oil Can" because it sounds like Earl Gann, and he doesn't object. I am sure he has a sense of humor and I look forward to many delightful moments with him.

The first day he came to work he told me about finding two dead Canada geese in the middle of the road. They were a male and a female and they bore no marks of having been run over by an automobile; yet they had broken necks. I told him to eat them without worrying about the way they might have died, as I had already seen geese kill themselves in the following manner.

When ducks and geese alight at night, it seems, they often mistake wet pavements for quiet water, and the force of such a sudden stop has killed many a bird. I recall finding on an airport, a dozen dead canvasbacks that had cracked up during a rain the night before. I told this story to duck shooters who laughed me down, so I did a little research of my own and came up with some interesting information. There are certain towns in the northwest on the migratory route of geese, I learned, that turn out their street lights if it rains during the hours of overnight alighting. One place had fifty-two dead geese in its town square after a rain.

But my friends still doubted. "Sloane," they said, "if you knew anything about ducks, you'd know how they land in water. They don't fly in at full speed; they slow down and plop into the water. How could that break a duck's neck?"

Well, their argument seemed right, so I went back to my research. Ducks, I learned, land differently at night than they do in the daytime. They do land "with full power on," if the night is dark. The object of this is so that they can take off again without having landed, if at the last instant they find an enemy in wait. Once a bird has lost flying speed, the business of landing, getting back into take-off position and again gaining flying speed takes up a dangerous lot of time. Earl believes my story but his wife still doubts, so there will be no goose on the Gann menu this week.

A few days ago I talked to Earl about taking the barn down. As I viewed it with its mantle of white, I realized that it must have held the snow of many winters on its sloping shoulders, and this is to be its last. The side boards are very wide—some over twenty-one inches—yet they are not warped. I shall certainly keep them and use them as they are, in the house. The wash given them by the rain and sun of two hundred summers and winters has rendered them with a better finish than anything I could do. I have already ripped off a few of these boards to panel the kitchen cupboard, and so many people have asked me how I got such a beautiful finish on the wood that I dreamed up a stock answer. "God knows," is my reply. "I don't."

The Christmas season seems officially dead when you dispose of your Christmas tree. But I got a small potted tree this year with the thought of planting it later. One should not transplant directly from the heat of the house to the cold of winter; the tree should first be left outside for a month, in the pot. This I have done, and today I transplanted the tree. If you have ever looked out at the bare trees on a cold night and wondered where winter birds rest, you might be interested to know that they usually take to these evergreens. I recall the wording on an ancient sampler that said:

God willed the firs to keep their green,
So birds might nest on Christmas E'en.

One of the most satisfying things that a man can do, it seems, is to plant a tree. The planting of this tree starts what I hope to be a line of Christmas trees at Weather Hill.

Because I have seen Christmas-tree balls made in the early 1800's and I know that the Christmas tree was originated at that time by the Germans, I have often wondered if the enterprising manufacturers of decorations had anything to do with the popularizing of Christmas trees. What an improvement to the idea if everyone who uses a cut-down Christmas tree planted one instead!

The weather has become colder, more like winter. This I realized very much when I dug the hole into frozen ground to transplant my tree. My outdoor thermometer has registered five below zero on two nights so far. Reports from the city, however, seem to indicate that it has been even colder there, and this brings up an interesting point. It has always been considered natural for the suburbs to be colder than the city, yet no one has yet dared to presume that man has had anything to do with this difference. I do believe that the taking away of green foliage and replacing it with cement has a great deal to do with temperature and weather. The fact that when everything is covered with snow there is less temperature difference between city and country seems to prove this point. The thousands of heating systems, the running of automobile motors and the general radiation of heat, even from the bodies of millions of human beings, must add up to some heat importance.

Another interesting reason why the surrounding country-side is often cooler than the city is that a breeze is stirred by the air that flows toward the city to replace the rising heat there.

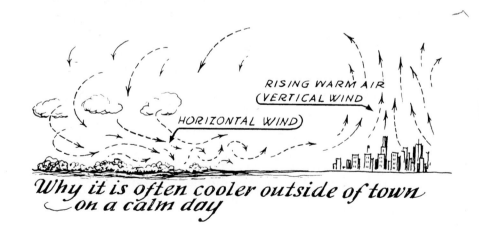

RISING WARM AIR
(VERTICAL WIND

HORIZONTAL WIND)

Why it is often cooler outside of town on a calm day

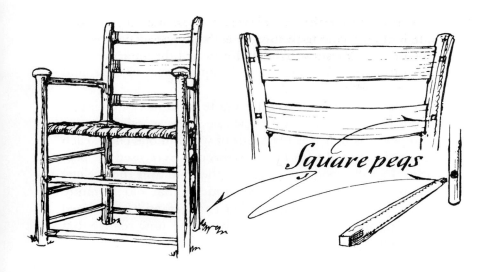

Square pegs

You NEVER KNOW where information will come from. This week it came from the barn, where an old chair frame that was cast aside had ended. Jimmy the farmer, who was chopping scrap wood there, asked me if I wanted it. "That," he added, "is a Powers chair." I told him to chop it up because it was rotted: but what, I wanted to know, was a "Powers chair"? "Well you just try to pull them joints apart," he said, "and you'll know." I tried, and found that although the wood was aged into uselessness, the joints themselves were like solid plastic. It didn't take me long to find out more about Powers chairs, as most of the farm folk still have them in their households.

Benjamin Powers of Lyndon, Vermont, started making chairs in 1814 when his father accused him of being a "square peg in a round hole." The idea of a square peg in a round hole didn't seem too bad to Ben, and that became his secret for making chair joints fit tight, and his advertising slogan. Besides this theory, he had further inventive carpentry genius. He joined green wood to dry wood in such a way that they soon welded together for all time. The factory has long disintegrated from the scene at Hawkins Brook in East Lyndon, and many of the chairs are disintegrating too. But the "welded" square pegs in the round holes will be last to go.

Today, furniture is usually made from just one kind of wood. In the old days when people knew wood, however, there were as many as ten kinds of wood in one chair, each having its special use. The hard woods were used for pegging, the soft woods for cradling the load and the springy woods for carrying it. I have noticed that old furniture creaks and cracks during weather changes, and I presumed it was because of age or weakness. But I now realize that the wooden things which tend to creak are those that have lasted longest, and their creaking has much to do with their longevity. Wood, it seems, reacts greatly to weather changes, warping, contracting, expanding, and "breathing" with every change in humidity and temperature. The object of the early craftsmen was to match woods that react in an opposite manner and thereby keep the joints tight. So the creaking you hear in an old house during weather changes is no defect; it is the natural breathing of old wood as one piece settles comfortably against another.

There has been a lot of house-creaking during the last twelve hours and I notice that the barometer is going down in an irregular manner. Last night the thermometer dipped near zero, but the weather has settled off warmer with skies becoming more webby and ceilinglike in structure, a fair indication of an approaching warm front. A warm front, of course, means a long, slow precipitation. This time, I think it will be snow.

One of our oldest and most relied-upon sky signs has been the sailor's "mackerel sky." Yet to me it is meaningless. I always remember the ditty, "Mackerel scales and mares' tails make lofty ships carry low sails," yet I have found the most perfect examples of such skies to bring neither wind nor rain.

Most people get cirro-cumulus (mackerel sky) and alto-cumulus confused. Alto-cumulus is simply an overall pattern of cumulus clouds. The cloud lumps of alto-cumulus look small because they are so high; they look close together for the same reason. Alto-cumulus is called sheep-herd sky because it looks like a herd of fluffy white lumps. But cirro-cumulus or "mackerel" clouds are much higher, finer, more indefinite and look exactly like rippled sand. If you associate cirro-cumulus with rippled sand, and alto-cumulus with herds of sheep, you will never get the two confused.

Weather wisdom starts with remembering and jotting down notes about what the sky looks like and what the barometer and thermometer are doing. To many people, all clouds look alike, but when you get the habit of the upward glance, you will find nothing more delicate and changing than the sky.

I had a friend who was chief of the Weather Bureau, and his unusual memory was respected by all. Yet it was simply the result of constantly recording notes. I once tested him by asking him if he remembered what the weather was on Easter a year ago, and he immediately told me that it rained during the evening. "But I remember that," he added, "because I left my umbrella in church."

Farmer Wanzer dropped by and delighted me with his rare choice of words. I will not call his language "New England" because there is often a tinge of ridicule in referring to anyone as a typical New Englander. Fifty years ago the American farmer was supposed to be the same sort of character that the New Englander is often regarded as being now. I enjoy the rich use of hand-me-down language that the New England farmer uses, but find it no indication that he thinks any differently than anyone else.

Wanzer, for example, never refers to weather or wind as being "bad," as most of us do; he uses instead the word "fearful." "Winters about here," he said, "were at one time fearful; now they ain't worth a pinch of snuff."

I have tried to remember the colorful words and phrases that the farmers here use, and rather than lose them I copy them down on a pad that I keep in my workshop. Here are some from my collection:

He gets more words from a breath than the average.

Getting cusseder and cusseder.

It won't do a bit of hurt.

As ripe as spring.

Farmer Wanzer says that the springs are flowing even before the snow melts, which is sign of an early spring. I certainly look forward to that season, for February has always been a stark and colorless month to me.

February is the season of blacks and whites. What color there is in the ground and in the sky is overshadowed by the crisp brilliance of light and shadow. The low clouds seem to reflect the deep wet colorings of earth, while the brilliant sunlight makes cloud shadows all the darker.

I have always been amused when people remark about the shafts of sunlight that often break through the clouds, saying, "Look—the sun is drawing water!" Actually sunlight *always* draws water into the air; this is the process of evaporation. Where there is shade, however, there is less evaporation. So people could rightly refer to the dark shafts of shadow among clouds and more accurately say, "Look—the sun is *not* drawing water!"

SUN DRAWING WATER (EVAPORATION)
SUN NOT DRAWING WATER (SHADE)

50

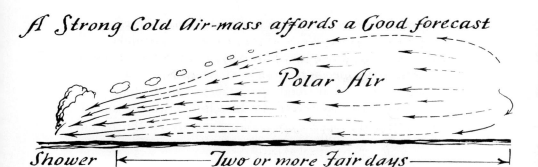

A Strong Cold Air-mass affords a Good forecast

Polar Air

Shower | ——————Two or more Fair days——————|

LAST NIGHT the wind shifted abruptly to the west and a flurry of snow skirted past the window, some striking the pane with a crisp tinkle. This change to a fair prevailing wind and the dryness of the snow were signs of a cold air mass.

It was not yet midnight so I chanced a telephone call to Mr. Miller, who had promised to paint the outside of Weather Hill when the first dry weather arrived. I told him the snow was just a momentary cold front and assured him that there would be at least two perfect days ahead for painting. He said he'd come.

Sure enough, when Miller arrived the morning skies were swept clean and there was a steady flow of air from the northwest. Here and there were the very small puffs of cumulus clouds such as usually ride the tail of a strong cold front.

When you paint on a wet day or during a warm air mass, you seal in the moisture of the day; a cool dry day is the painter's best friend.

Miller is a man of unusual dignity, yet he is a quick, efficient worker. He pleased me at once, and I added him to my "finds" of interesting New England people. But I learned that he has just moved to Connecticut and comes from the very part of Long Island where I had lived.

While he is around the house and I can use his long

ladder, I shall go about the business of trimming the trees around the house. Nothing will rot a house quicker than nearby trees. This I knew already, but the truth was impressed upon me more than ever when I chopped down two apple trees that stood twenty feet from the forge barn. There across the roof were two blotches of decayed shingles that extended down the side, looking exactly like the shadows of the two trees. The trees had actually cast a "shadow" of decaying moisture.

Early farmhouses had few trees around them except for one large tree, usually a pine. Pine is oily, carrying less dampness in its foliage; its needles actually help preserve old shingle roofs. Many of the ancient farm buildings have a pine-needle matting on their roofs heavier than the shingles they cover.

An old book about farming advises the removal of trees on the west side of the building, and the reason sounds logical. "When rain ends," it reads, "the clearing wind is usually from the west. Now who wants the west wind to continue splattering your barns with yesterday's moisture, even though the present skies are fair?"

While on the roof trimming the branches within reach, I saw in the distant sky a small round cloud that appeared first dark and then as a bright light, and I called Miller to witness it. For twenty minutes the thing stayed in the same place, growing black, disappearing for an instant then burning again like a bright light. We were at a loss to explain it until I got my field glasses. Then I could see that it was a flock of birds, turning in a tight circle. Head on, they became invisible, but going away broadside, they showed their dark wingspreads and made up a cloud of shaded figures. When they soared toward us, the sun glistened on the flock's wings and the "cloud" changed to brightness. Without glasses we never would have guessed what it was. I wondered how many similar explainable things have been passed off as flying saucers or supernatural phenomena.

I asked Miller how cold weather might affect new paint and he assured me that I had nothing to worry about. "The nights get down to zero here," he remarked, "but they are drier than on Long Island. I haven't had a three-blanket night yet." Miller is certainly taking to Yankeeism when he talks about a "three-blanket night." The people here seldom refer to actual temperature; they describe coldness by the number of blankets they need for keeping warm at night. Temperature hereabouts seems to range from "one-sheet nights" to "three-blanket nights."

In collecting Yankeeisms, I first tried to trace down the meaning of the word Yankee but found very little information. Webster agrees with an old legend about "Yankee" being the American Indians' unhappy effort to pronounce the word "English." They came out with something that sounded like "Yengees." The Dutch, in turn, thought the Indians' mispronunciation was something like their own word for John, which is Janke and is pronounced "Yon-cay." So the New York and Pennsylvania Dutch referred to the New Englanders as those "northern Johns," or as they would pronounce it, those northern "Yoncays."

The word Yankee has been used proudly and also in ridicule; mostly, I do believe, in ridicule. It was Dr. Schuckburgh, a British army surgeon, who wrote "Yankee Doodle" in ridicule of the shabbily dressed troops of Colonel Thomas Fitch of Norwalk, Connecticut. Elizabeth Fitch, so the story goes, was unhappy about the army dress of her brother, and saying, "You must have *some* sort of uniform," she ran into the barnyard before he left for duty, getting a long turkey feather for his hat. Fitch caught the humor of her act, and in true Yankee spirit took along feathers for all his troops. When Dr. Schuckburgh saw the feathered soldiers approaching, he sarcastically referred to them as "macaronis," which was slang of the day for "dude" or "dandy." Hence the famous lines, "stuck a feather in his hat and called him macaroni." Webster says that a doodle is a simple fellow or fop, so the term "Yankee Doodle" is in ridicule.

Seldom have I heard a Yankee call himself Yankee although I do recall a sampler supposed to have been sewed in 1738 which went:

Mary Kendall is my name, Yankeeland my nation;
Wyndham is my dwelling place and Christ is my salvation.

And on a Connecticut tombstone of 1770:

. . . in Yankee ground I choose to be,
and dwell with Saints eternally.

My dog Nimbo came in tonight covered with burs, and was very grateful for my removing them. I'd often wondered what mechanism causes burs to stick so stubbornly, and thought it might be interesting to look at them under a magnifying glass. Between the glass and research in my nature library, I am now all the wiser for Nimbo's collection of burs. There are actually sharp hooks on the end of each needle, I found, and they are designed so beautifully that I am surprised they can be torn loose at all.

Plants that drop seeds are in a way competing with themselves, but burs such as black snakeroot, beggar's tick, tick trefoil and cocklebur have the advantage of giving their seeds the ability to "hitchhike" to distant places. All of us have at some time or other carried burs miles away from where they grew, just as nature intended.

The Black Snakeroot bur looks like this

The Beggar's Tick looks like this

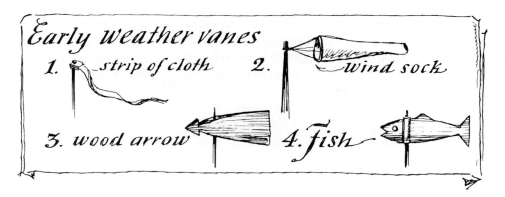

Early weather vanes
1. strip of cloth   2. wind sock
3. wood arrow   4. fish

THE WINDY MONTH of March is rushing the season, for here in the last week of February the wind has been strong and gusty throughout each day. Weather Hill is within a slight hollow of hilltop, which accounts for the gustiness and has discouraged me from erecting a weather vane. The direction of the wind and its tendency to change are the most important factors in weather prediction. I must depend upon watching the clouds' direction of movement, which is more accurate but often difficult.

The first weather vanes were strips of cloth. In fact the word "vane" comes from the Anglo-Saxon word "fano," flag, and the earliest wind vanes were more properly known as "winde-fanos" or wind-flags. The next development in weather vanes was the wind sock, which we still use at airports. This was designed in Scotland when golf was in the "featherball" stage and the slightest wind had a great deal to do with where the ball went.

The first weather vanes of America were made of very light and dry white pine, which is probably the reason why there are none surviving today. They were in the form of an arrow, a hand, or a fish. The cocks and horses did not show up until the metal vanes appeared.

The so-called ancient American weather vanes are not as old as we may think, for when America was young, it was considered vulgar to place ornaments on the home or the barn. Only when Pennsylvania became developed, and the German tradition of barn-embellishment became popular, was the big metal weather vane recognized as standard farm equipment Some of the Pennsylvania weather vanes were too heavy for anything but the strongest wind to move, although they served their purpose to "pretty up the barn."

Windy nights are often clear ones, and tonight the sky is cloudless and the stars are bright and twinkly. Twinkling stars, I recall, are signs of rain. This fluctuation of light is caused mainly by irregular refraction due to great inequalities in the upper atmosphere. And such instability aloft will usually lower to earth in time, in the form of rain or snow.

While watching the stars, I saw the blinking lights of an airliner passing over Connecticut on its Boston run. I remembered a letter written to the little Methodist Church in Georgetown, from an airline pilot. "A night pilot gets pretty lonely," it read, "and it makes me feel warm inside to see your steeple light when I'm nearing my destination in New York. It's a landmark I always look for. Enclosed find ten dollars donation to your fund for lighting the church." There is never any name signed to the letter but a similar one arrives every year.

The most important date in the last week of February is Washington's birthday. When Weather Hill was young, few people knew when Washington was born; but now, when we have more or less forgotten Washington's accomplishments, we all know the day he was born. My neighbor Tebell has written a fine book about Washington's life. He told me about mentioning in his book the time that the General was the first passenger to cross nearby Bull's Bridge. This is the legend they still tell around here, relating how Mr. Bull had not yet finished the bridge and how he led Washington's horse across the bare stringers, and refused to accept the toll of two cents. But inasmuch as the earliest known covered bridge was built after 1800 (the present

Bull's Bridge is covered), and was built to accommodate Civil War troops, I wonder if the years have not confused the tongues of the storytellers. I do believe that Washington did cross an earlier uncovered bridge, near the present Bull's Bridge. This event was so glorified, I suspect, that the story continued long after the destruction of the old bridge and attached itself to the newer covered bridge. Yet the tale has made Bull's Bridge famous, and I must admit I like it myself.

Oddly enough, I have gone many miles to "discover" hidden-away covered bridges, and have not yet inspected Bull's Bridge, which is so close by. For those who enjoy antiquity, there is nothing better to break the monotony of a long motor tour than to seek out covered bridges along the way. It will usually lead you to the quaintest countryside and most attractive back-river landscapes.

A shorter and more convenient break to the monotony of a superhighway is to explore the remains of the old original road that frequently are seen jutting away from the new concrete road, sometimes disappearing into the countryside and then returning to the highway. I wonder who takes care of those abandoned roads. Motoring to New York last week, I left the highway to follow a bit of abandoned road that was left to wind into the hills when a new bridge came into existence, and I found the curves of yesteryear to my liking. There were several old farmhouses and one place that bore evidences of having been an inn. I saw a pheasant disappear into the underbrush and while I stopped the car to investigate, I became aware of a deer that had frozen himself to stillness, watching me from the edge of the woods. I shall make this detour a part of my trip to the city whenever time permits.

Some day someone will dream up the idea of building such country roads for people who enjoy the countryside but don't want to go anywhere. On the highways, particularly on holidays, people are out for nothing but the sensation of movement; if they slow up to look at the landscape they endanger those behind who have some place to go, so much of the scenery goes to waste. I suggest dirt roads with country stores that will not be "bettered" by supermarkets, a lot of old barns and covered bridges, and all the puddles and road hazards of fifty years ago. A lot of people would pay a dollar to ride on such a road. Perhaps some of those old bypassed and deserted roads might be made into one of these country parkways.

February has my vote for being the bleakest month. But the fireside is all the more inviting, and I find it easier to work and paint then. It has been said that most of the great works of writing and art found their expression during February. Perhaps the idea of people feeling brisker during winter truly means that in a cold and dismal world, we would rather work than do anything else.

In sending our inquiries about old almanacs, I unearthed a sort of superalmanac that was devised by Frederick Gleason in 1850. The *Life* magazine of its day, *Gleason's Pictorial* made its publisher fabulously rich in four years. But when he then sold the paper to his editor, the *Pictorial* soon dropped out of sight and Gleason died a poor man. The format of the *Pictorial* was that of the almanacs, a sort of parlor companion of news, timely articles and household hints; it was printed weekly and made to be bound into yearly volumes. I notice in February's news that an autograph of Washington's Farewell Address sold for twenty-three hundred dollars. That sum in 1850 would be equal to a fortune today.

I also found an article about the effect of weather on fishing. It is my opinion that weather affects the fisherman more than it does the fish, but many of the old-timers around here disagree. They insist that fish bite best when the moon is in its first quarter. They also say that "when the barometer begins to rise, so do the fish." So if you put those two pieces of fish lore together and wait for a barometric rise during the moon's first quarter, you should certainly be assured of good fishing.

Here is a calendar compiled by one of the local farmers, based on notes which his father took from an old almanac. These things that you cannot completely believe or disbelieve have a way of lingering in your memory, so I suppose I shall some day try it out.

The 63 Best fishing days of the year

Jan.	Feb.	Mar.	Apr.	May	Jun.	July	Aug.	Sep.	Oct.	Nov.	Dec.
17	13 14 15	12 13 14	9 10 28 29	16 25 26	16 25 26		13 23 24	9 10 11 19 20	8 9 10	5 6	3 4

Morning   Evening

Jan.	Feb.	Mar.	Apr.	May	Jun.	July	Aug.	Sep.	Oct.	Nov.	Dec.
8 19 16 18	6	22	18 20	6 7 17	3 4 22	1 17 18 19 20	14 15 16	12 13	17	13 14 15	11 12 30

If you believe in this sort of thing, do match this calendar with a Rising Barometer!

59

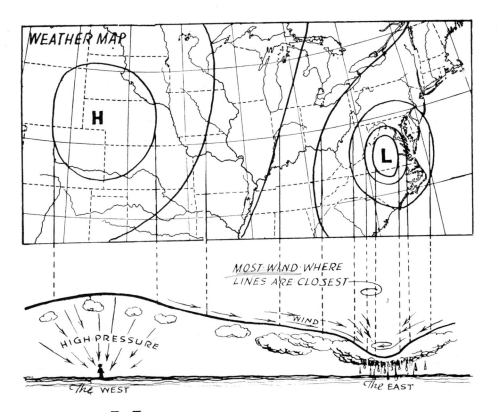

WEATHER MAP

MOST WIND WHERE LINES ARE CLOSEST

HIGH PRESSURE

WIND

The WEST

The EAST

First Week of March

My barograph has been high but unsteady. The inked line looks like the contour of a mountain range. Oddly enough, the barograph, in measuring the pressure of air above it, really does map out mountains of atmospheric density. I presume that the steep "hills" indicated on the line of my chart explain the erratic winds outside. Wind, I guess, is very much like a river of motion, flowing by gravity down hills of its own density. The bigger the pressure drop, the greater the wind.

I have often wondered why newspaper weather maps have never had a simpler explanation accompanying them. So many people turn to the map even before reading the news, although they have not the slightest idea of what the map portrays. Most everyone knows what a geographical contour map is and how its lines map out the elevation of hills and valleys. So if it were explained that a weather map is identical to a geographical map, except that it outlines hills (highs) and sinkholes (lows) of atmospheric density, the weather map would have much more meaning to so many.

√March is known for its wind, but I do believe that the bareness of the trees, and the resulting whine and howl throughout the forest, has a great deal to do with the fame of March winds. All the old almanacs start this month with a poetical piece about wind. My oldest one says, "Blow winds and crack your cheeks; rage, blow! You cataracts and hurricanes, spout till you have drench'd our steeples and drown'd the cocks."

Being near a crackling fireplace and hearing the March wind whine past the chimney is a great treat—they make fine background music for an evening of dreaming into the past. Wind and rain are the music of weather: rain is the percussion instrument that sets the rhythm while wind carries the melody. All rain sounds the same to me, just as all drums do; but winds are as different as one song is from another. You can often tell the time of the year by the sound of the wind. Then there are winds that belong to places, just like folk music. Alaska's williwaw, China's typhoon and the Rocky Mountains' chinook are part of their landscape. The winds of some distant places are as romantic as their history, and the names of the winds are as rich and suggestive as the names of faraway lands. The chubasco, chocolatero, siffanto, tormento, the solano and mistral and elephanta and countless others are winds that are as much a part of their native countries as anything else.

"A new moon and a windy night," an old New England saying goes, "sweeps cobwebs out of the drab house of February." Wind has been responsible for much thawing, and despite snow flurries from the low-hanging stratocumulus clouds, spring cannot be far away. You cannot feel it in the air yet, but you can sense it just over the horizon.

The woodpile that I thought would last the winter is now gone. In the country an empty woodpile is like an empty wallet. Jimmy the farmer has begun collecting branches and limbs that the winds have felled, so that neighbor Carlson may come by with his power saw and cut them up. It is such a pleasure to work with Carlson, feeding the whining saw, hearing it slow up when the wood becomes harder or when a knot is encountered, smelling the good wood odor that has been locked inside for many years. A woodpile, a library and a pantry shelf have much in common, all stocked with material for man's comfort. But the oldest and most essential is the woodpile.

Earl Gann has started to take the old barn down and there is much firewood in it, seasoned by two hundred years of weather. Yet I cannot ask Carlson to risk his saw blade on building wood full of handmade spikes and nails. Some of the barn timbers have become so hard with age that a saw draws smoke from them and you almost expect to see sparks fly. I once brought some old barn timbers from Wilton, Connecticut, to Brookfield, Long Island, to grace my living-room ceiling; now I find myself using the same type of precious material for firewood. Some day while there is still a store of ancient and seasoned wood in the remaining barns that are scattered in the back country, a smart contractor will buy it up.

It is interesting to note how many things you can tell about a man by observing his barn. The first owner of Weather Hill was a very tall man, for the small sawed-off tree crotches used for hanging harnesses in the barn were placed close to seven feet from the floor. He was a considerate man, for he'd contrived a little swinging door for the barn cat to go in and out through. He liked his blackberry brandy, for the jug was still there on a beam with a groove worn into the wood from the many times the jug had been taken down and then slid back into place. He was a smoking man, too, for there were scratches from many years of match-lighting on the door frame, again at such a height as to indicate the reach of a tall man. And he had a pair of hands like hams, for their imprints are on some of the plaster that was found between the foundation and the sills: my own hand looks like a baby's when I compare it.

Earl Gann told me that he found a chipmunk nest beneath the barn sills and that he startled the occupants from their last hours of hibernation. Although one chipmunk was awake and active, it rolled over and feigned death after the manner of an opossum. I wonder how many animals have this strange protective habit. Insects and spiders feign death; so do reptiles. The hog-nosed snake turns on its back and, with its tongue hanging out, looks as if it has died after some terrible torture. The great mistake it makes is that if you turn it over to its normal position, it will immediately roll over again and play dead.

There is evidence of the vegetation coming out of its hibernation too. In the valley there are pussy willows and skunk cabbages pushing through patches of snowy ground, and muskrats are already feeding along the shores of the lake, wherever the ice has sufficiently broken up.

This week I learned something interesting about clouds. While making photographs of the old barn as it was being dismantled, I took a picture of a fine fair-weather cumulus cloud as it floated over the scene. When the negatives returned from the photo-finishers, the fair-weather cloud, which was then in reverse, had an angry and stormy appearance. It occurred to me that an artist could make his clouds appear stormy by simply doing a negative or reverse-shadowed sketch of them. I tried it and the results were good. I guess that during stormy turbulence, the light from within clouds is stronger than the light from the outside atmosphere, and highlights and shadows tend to change place.

"positive" "negative"

(a fair-weather cloud and an "Angry" one)

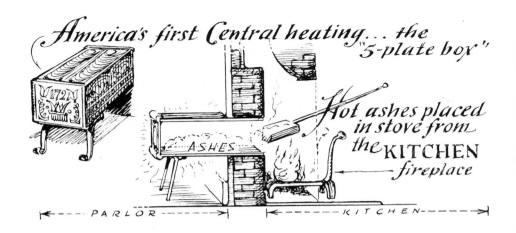

America's first Central heating... the "5-plate box"

Hot ashes placed in stove from the KITCHEN fireplace

ASHES

|← - - - - PARLOR - - - - - - →| |← - - - - - - KITCHEN - - - - - →|

Second
Week
of
March

THESE ARE THE MORNINGS when a wood stove becomes a great pleasure. I do not know exactly why, but the heat of burning wood is more than just heat. Whereas coal heat seems to glow steadily into a room, wood heat dances. Its light, its sound and its smell delight the senses. A wood fire's flame lights the room with cheerfulness; its sound is lively, from the popping and crackling of dry pine to the wheezing and whistling of steaming green oak; its smell is a joy that becomes added spice to whatever you cook over it.

I never light my Franklin stove without silently saluting the great man who devised it. Benjamin Franklin did so many things expertly, including being the foremost meteorologist of his time. The Franklin stove is a result of his very fine knowledge of air currents: his cross-section drawings of storms display the same theory that is pronounced in his plans for the stove. His drawings explaining hurricanes are still used with very little change. Franklin would certainly be an expert in air conditioning if he lived today.

After an eclipse of the moon, Franklin noticed in a Boston newspaper account that the sky of that night had become clouded by a northeast storm about five hours later than the same thing had occurred in Philadelphia. He immediately sent for newspapers of that day from cities all over the coast, and by compiling their accounts and marking them upon a map, he made America's first authentic weather map. The most interesting thing about Franklin's map, however, was that winds did not blow from the storm center but around it. This led him to choose a group of weather-minded friends, living in scattered locations, whom he asked to keep a weather diary with him. By making daily wind maps, he substantiated his theory that wind blows counterclockwise around low-pressure areas.

Weather Hill, unfortunately, was a modern farmhouse of its day. It was built when iron stoves were being designed to replace the fireplace, and variations of the Franklin stove were being made in all the nearby Connecticut iron mills. Only in the kitchen and living room were there fireplaces, one backing up against the other. The main chimney, which protruded from the center of the roof, started oddly enough in the attic. It is still there, although a new roof has been built over it; pipes were led into this chimney from the various rooms, and the heat from several "modern Connecticut stoves" probably were the envy of the surrounding farmhouses that were heated with conventional fireplaces. I do not know where the original stoves from Weather Hill are now, but I have found broken stove plates thrown into some of the stone walls around the house, so I presume that they cracked and broke from use and age.

The earliest American stoves were only five cast-iron plates that went together by grooves or straps to form a box fed from a fireplace in the adjoining room. When Franklin invented a detached fireplace in 1744, the warming box began to disappear. But not without resentment. "Despite their usefulness," reads one account, "they are criticised. If the chimney cannot be swept, there is danger of fire. Some think the stoves give too much heat. The Germans will keep to their warming boxes for they cost less."

From the beginning, stove makers have put strange embellishments and colorful names on their stoves. One of the pieces of stove plate that I found in a stone wall behind the barn has an acorn design on it, and it sports the name Uncle Daniel. I have seen more recent stoves with such names as Parlor Queen, Little Willie, Pearl, Home Sunshine, Nuthatch and Vesuvius. This practice, I do believe, started when the early ironmasters began naming their furnaces after the women in their family. Elizabeth, the name of one furnace run by "Baron" Stiegel of Pennsylvania, was named for his wife; the stove plates from this furnace also bear the name Elizabeth. Some of the Baron's stove plates even sport lengthy Biblical quotations in Latin and German.

The Franklin-type stoves had less ornamentation, perhaps a blazing sun with the traditional face in the middle, but the name of the maker became less conspicuous, often placed in the back of the stove. Some models had flat tops and storage tanks on the side for water; you could cook on top, obtain hot water from the side, see the fire in front and get heat from the whole contraption. Not bad.

One advantage that stoves have over fireplaces is the fact that gusts of wind will not backfire ashes into the room. These March winds have been doing just that at Weather Hill. The strange thing about March winds is that they do not die down at sunset as good winds are supposed to do, but they keep beating away, gusts and all.

Today there was a great deal of dust blown into the air from the barren ground. What a pity that sand and gravel pits have invaded the Connecticut countryside. As I went to town today, I saw clouds of dust being blown from the ugly scars in the hillside made by the gravel companies. Neighbor Wanzer has just sold his tobacco field for a gravel pit. He is old and he has had the pleasure of seeing his fields grow green and produce; but those left behind will inherit only wounds on the face of the land that will remain until all the fields and the farms are gone.

Those who have flown and are familiar with the landmarks that a flier looks for will know about sand and gravel pits and how they become a part of the aviation map—always growing in size, always bare. I tried to explain this to Wanzer but he tells me that this sort of thing is progress. "The land," he says, "wasn't bringing in enough money as a farm." I wanted to tell him that poverty is not the money we fail to get, but the beauty we fail to see. A farmer of two hundred years ago, I think, would have understood.

Neighbor Carlson, too, has a cancerous scar on his farm. "The gravel man paid me more than that rocky land could have grown in corn. More money than I could have made in five years. That's *prosperity*," he told me. Those are disappointing words to one who has moved to Connecticut to become part of the landscape and to adopt the New Englander's love of land.

The New England farmer of today has inherited land cleared the hard way with rocks carried by hand or by ox sled, and piled meticulously into the walls that have lasted for more than two centuries. To see the cycle of growing fields stopped, and the old walls eaten away by bulldozers, I should think, would be too much for a true farmer to witness.

"*Only in New England can they throw stones in a pile and have it come out a Wall.*"
B. Franklin

---- pit
Round stones inside
Flat stones slanted on outside

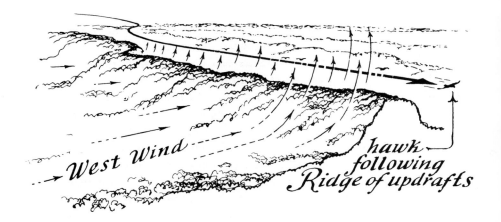

West Wind

hawk following Ridge of updrafts

Third Week of March

THE MELTING SNOW brings out strong moist thermals to fill the March sky with billowy cumulus clouds, making it look very much like summer overhead. Winter atmosphere thins out from the density of near earth to the thinness of near space in a very uniform and gradual manner; but the atmosphere of warm weather is full of irregularities and vertical winds.

One time I built a set of weather models for the American Museum of Natural History to depict cross sections through atmospheric phenomena: I used moving blue lights to represent descending cold air and red lights to show rising warm air. If air were actually colored, the atmosphere of winter would thin out smoothly, but March skies would begin to appear splotchy and streaked with the irregular currents of heat thermals.

This morning I saw several hawks soaring over toward the lake, and sensed that there were a number of thermals rising from the water. The flying books taught me that updrafts were over land and downdrafts over water; but now I have learned that at certain times there is warmer air rising from water. It seems that when a cold air mass sweeps by, water retains its heat a little longer than land; and for a brief period a lake will issue strong thermals, like warm bubbles bursting through the river of cooler air.

You could see the hawks circle tightly within the invisible bubble of rising air, and flap back into it whenever they slipped outside the magic updraft. Most people think that winds all blow horizontally, but the sky is frothing with up and down winds too. And the top of each strong upward wind is usually capped by a cumulus cloud as the air's moisture breaks from invisible vapor to visible droplets.

Sometimes vertical winds have nothing to do with heat circulation but are caused by the air bouncing off low-altitude obstacles, such as pockets of dense air or sudden rises of mountain heights. In Pennsylvania, the mountain ranges run in long rows of ridges, often at a right angle to the prevailing wind. This causes a steady bouncing off and upward current of air, sometimes for a hundred miles or more. More interesting still is that this aerial roadway of updrafts is in the direct route of migrating hawks. Hawks by the hundreds get aboard for a free ride and take the long trip, often without flapping their wings for miles at a time.

This seems to be a season of wet winds. If I were to picture March in my mind's eye, there would be a pool of water in a muddy road, whipped into ripples by the wind. Reflected in the water would be gray clouds of the changing season, and I would not be certain if the puddle came from rain or melted snow.

March twentieth is the first day of spring. On this day I walked around my land and wondered if there is any connection between the word "spring" and the multitude of springs that seem to gush at this time. On less than one acre, I counted twelve bubbling streams bursting through the thawed ground.

The site of Weather Hill, like the site of all old farmhouses, was chosen for its proximity to a good spring. Before the time of pumps, it must have been pleasant to watch the never-ceasing flow of water as it trickled into the big kitchen spring barrel. Farmer Wanzer at the foot of the hill has all modern conveniences in his house, but he still prefers the spring barrel and he has plastic and chromium counters running right up to the rim of the same barrel that was there when he was a child. I have never felt any great pleasure in getting water from a faucet, despite the wonders of present-day plumbing; but I think I'd get great satisfaction and comfort from a kitchen spring. The pipes from an old spring still lead to Weather Hill but I do not know where they lie. Wanzer tells me that I might locate them with a divining rod.

A few of the old-timers still use divining rods to "witch" water or locate springs underground. When they hold a forked willow stick with both hands and walk slowly around a well site, a mysterious pull is supposed to exert itself and pull the point of the V toward the nearest water. The divining rod is also used to locate underground tiles, hidden pipes, hidden treasure or whatever the witcher has faith in it to do.

One of the local well diggers has devised a chromium divining rod. It is made from two welding rods, three-sixteenths of an inch thick and three feet long. After six-inch handles are bent in the rods, and when they are held broom-fashion with the long parts horizontal to the ground and a few inches apart, the rods are supposed to come together when you are above a "find." He says he uses it as a gag, but still it is part of his equipment and I wonder how much of a gag it really is. He copied the plans, incidentally, from a 1954 almanac which gives complete specifications for making and using it.

I asked Earl Gann where I could find a man to witch my hidden spring pipes, and he tells me that "most witchers has died off," but he did tell me something of great interest that I have never seen written. He explained that in early times the hazel tree was used only for making divining rods, because there was supposed to be something mystic about that tree. Its blossoms smell like the area about a spring, and it blooms when its leaves are faded and falling, in the autumn.

So, many years ago, the hazel tree was known as the witch tree or witch-hazel tree. I never guessed that the witch hazel used for sprains and aches had any connection with divining rods.

One of the untrue sayings of folklore is that trees with much moss are always near a spring. The reason for moss on a tree is that the sun has not been able to reach that part, and the moisture has collected there. This usually occurs at the base of the tree, where water falls by its own weight, and on the north side, where the sun strikes least. In fact, if you are lost on a sunless day, you can usually locate north by observing the moss at the bases of the trees.

One of the true sayings of folklore, however, is that a heavy dew late at night is a sign of a good day on the morrow. I seldom find a dry night that isn't followed by precipitation the following day. When the night air is clear and has few nuclei for cloud particles to form upon, it seems, moisture frees itself most readily from the air and collects as dew. But when the night sky is full of cloud particles and has the makings of a cloudy and rainy day tomorrow, it is spongelike in its ability to retain moisture, and there is little or no dew.

These mornings, before the sun is up, I find that the dew is in the form of hoarfrost. Hoarfrost is actually not frozen dew, but the moisture of air deposited in solid form without first having passed into the liquid state.

This week I raked my first leaves of the year, which is my favorite way to work up an appetite in the morning. While the coffee is perking inside the house, and the air outside is perfumed by the tang of burning leaves, there is no better way to start the day.

I have never been quite sure whether the smell of burning leaves should be associated with spring or fall. It makes me think of spring. Childhood impressions are lasting ones, and to this day I remember the times my father would take me to our summer place when he opened it in early spring. This was the time for taking down storm doors and raking the leaves of winter away from the house—always an event for early rising. The smell of burning leaves and coffee seem to go together; it is a joy that I shall never tire of.

My favorite doorman is Mr. Terwilliger at the Hotel Biltmore in New York. He told me once that he used to be a gardener on a Long Island estate, and that when spring fills the air, he becomes very lonely for the country. But once a year he motors out to Long Island by himself; he brushes up a stack of leaves and burns them. Then, he tells me, he returns to the city feeling better.

My favorite leaf is the sassafras leaf. Its proportions are varied, yet they are always beautifully symmetrical. The sassafras is the only tree that I know of which has three entirely different kinds of leaves on each branch. One is an oval-shaped leaf, another is shaped like a mitten, while the third has three oval fingers. From root to leaf, the sassafras is stored with flavor, and I always enjoy chewing on a sassafras twig when walking through the countryside.

There seems something distinctly American about the sassafras tree. It was one of our first exports, and the first Englishman to set foot on our New England shores was Captain Gosnold, who landed at Cape Cod in 1602 to procure a cargo of sassafras for medicinal purposes. The roots of this tree were said to have great powers of health, and sassafras tea was a daily drink of the first settlers. Tales went back to England about the recuperative powers of the tea, and before long sassafras root was the New World's most valuable article of commerce. How odd that one seldom hears of it now.

The three sassafras leaves

1.   2.   3.

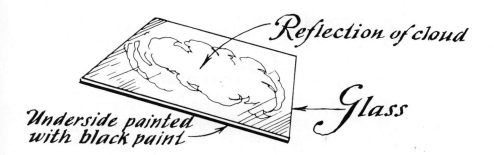

Reflection of cloud

Glass

Underside painted with black paint

THE MARCH WINDS are dying down. My dog Nimbo and I walked to the lake to see if all the ice had disappeared. There were still traces on the opposite shore but otherwise the lake was like a sheet of glass. The reflection of clouds in the water was more beautiful than the sky itself, and it reminded me of my black-glass contraption for cloud-watching. The idea of using a black-glass, which I thought was new, proved to be old: in Loomis's *Meteorology*, printed in 1862, I found it saying, "The best way to view the sky is to look at its reflection in a sheet of black glass. We are thus able to detect peculiarities which entirely escape observations made by the unassisted eye." My glass, however, is merely a pane of window glass with the bottom side painted black. Yet it is remarkable how different the clouds will appear in it, and how many new colors you can see without the glare of direct sunlight.

Nimbo, I am afraid, is getting on in years. He used to walk right through puddles but now he carefully detours around them. They say that a boy becomes a man when he walks around puddles instead of through them. I also notice how much more he misses seeing than he used to during our jaunts. Only when a squirrel runs along the branches or scolds him from close range does Nimbo really take notice. Squirrels are masters for choosing the right place on a tree to freeze into stillness and look like a bump on the bark. But Nimbo, whose eyes, like all dogs' eyes, are built to see movement rather than color and three dimensions as a human eye does, waits for the slightest movement to make the squirrel visible again. The least wind that ruffles the "frozen" squirrel's tail will give him away to the eye of a dog.

It is hard for us to imagine the seeing of movement alone, for movement is no more than the action of the three-dimensional things that we already see. But if you can imagine looking at a page of newsprint where one single letter was somehow made to move, you would then be seeing movement: you would not be able to read the whole page or be more than aware of its existence before your eyes, but you would see very well the exact way that one letter was moving. As my dog Nimbo looks out of the picture window at Weather Hill, he often barks at the expanse of landscape, telling me in his dog language that he sees a cow, a man or a dog. If I look carefully, I can pick out the object, sometimes over a mile away, and I have often marveled at his ability to see so well. But remembering that dogs specialize in seeing movement, it is probably like that one moving letter on a page of newsprint.

Just a thousand feet away from Weather Hill and toward the lake, we came across some aged apple trees, and a few scattered lilac bushes. These two things, of course, always mark the place where an old farmhouse once stood. Sure enough, among the stones and underbrush I found the foundation for a small house. Such ruins seem to speak as plainly as words, and they almost ask the beholder to stop and listen. I sat there and tried to visualize the house, the view from its threshold and what it looked like when the apple trees were first planted there. More than likely they were planted from seed, for that was the custom. These trees are mere shells that have remained alive just by stubbornness and the ability to grow once more wherever a broken limb touched the ground and took root again.

I read in an almanac that Governor Endicott of Massachusetts traded five hundred three-year-old apple trees for two hundred and fifty acres of land: it seems that apple trees had great value to the early American. Another account is from Fort Vancouver in Oregon, in 1836. The writer was Mrs. Narcissa Whitman, and in her diary she wrote, "Here we find fruit of every description—apples, grapes, pears, plums, figs . . . all grown from seeds. A gentleman 12 years ago, while at a party in London, put seeds of the grapes and apples in his pocket. Soon afterward, he took a voyage to America. These seeds have now greatly multiplied."

I wonder how many of the trees planted by Johnny Appleseed remain. One was still alive at Stow, Ohio, in 1952. One of six apple trees, all over forty feet tall with trunks about four feet in diameter, it had been broken off into a twelve-foot stump, the last to remain. But even then, new suckers were appearing from the stump, and it looked as though Johnny Appleseed's work was still not finished within the frame of the old tree. Many monuments have been erected to Jonathan Chapman (Johnny Appleseed), but the best monuments were the trees that he planted.

I am afraid that I am too sentimental about old houses and the places where people have built and lived and died, for I feel sensitive to the past, and as most people "respect the dead," I become filled with respect for the things they did. I should like to build again right on the old foundation and make the apple trees and lilacs again a part of the farm.

It is strange how people respect death more than they respect life. I am sure that when I get my tombstone patio fixed and the old stones turned face up, there will be many guests who will be squeamish and tiptoe around the stones rather than step upon them. The only stone I have turned so far is marked Moses Allen, who died at ninety-four. I understand that he was the one who planed and laid the floors in Weather Hill. I am no more squeamish about walking on Moses's gravestone than I am about walking on the fine planks he laid. I think that Moses himself would be the first to agree with me.

I have been collecting the various ways for determining the antiquity of things. Graves around here, I find, faced the east before 1775, because of some superstition about the spirit rising toward the morning sun. I also learned that the wood-screw had no point on it before 1856, and I now have had great fun inspecting the screws in the doors at Weather Hill to learn their age. Most of the hinges were nailed with the nail bent over, which dates them before the nineteenth century.

HINGE

← *Eighteenth-century method*

BENT

Before 1856

After 1856

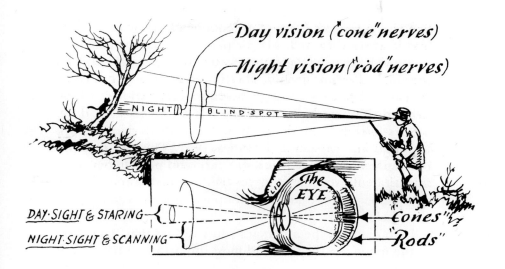

Day vision ("cone" nerves)

Night vision ("rod" nerves)

NIGHT BLIND·SPOT

The EYE

DAY·SIGHT & STARING

NIGHT·SIGHT & SCANNING

"Cones"

"Rods"

THE WEATHER has been unseasonably warm and the barometer is steady. Just at sundown I saw a string of geese flying northward. Winter's back is broken.

The old barn is down. Jimmy the farmer came by five hours after dark and, even before the moon had risen, worked until every beam was flat on the ground. I had just settled down to an evening by the fireplace when I heard a tremendous crash outside. I ran up the hill in the direction of the barn and found Jimmy hard at work. I had never before seen anyone working in the dark, particularly at work that would be dangerous even in daylight. But he assured me that everything was under control and that he did most of his odd jobs after dark.

"If you want to see things best at night, practice looking at them out of the side of your eye. Don't look square at anything," he said, "but just to one side of it. 'Possum hunting taught me that and I've practiced it ever since. Now I can see right good at night." He surely can. He told me further that he did some of his plowing at night, and all of his planting.

I tried Jimmy's method of looking at things after dark, and it works very well. My air pilot's manual explains that our eyes have two sets of nerves, one for night sight and the other for daytime seeing. Daytime sight is like a narrow flashlight beam, while night sight sees in a wide scope all around that beam. So if we stare at an object after dark, we are forced to use the narrow beam which doesn't work at night, and the object will disappear. This can be demonstrated by going out into the dark and picking out some faint star. By staring at it, you will see it disappear. Look just to one side of it and it will appear again, even brighter than before.

If you look at the almanacs you will find that the phases of the moon are the first and most important entry of each month. This, I presume, had something to do with illumination for night work, but more important was the practice of planting, felling trees and doing many of the chores of farm life according to certain phases of the moon. "Firewood cut in the last quarter of the moon of January," says one almanac, "will not throw embers out into your room." "Wood cut in the full of the moon," says another, "will most certainly not season well." Almost every kind of farm vegetable or grain had its superstition about what phase of the moon was best for planting it. Even the laying of shingles and the mixing of plaster had its moon folklore. So the moon information given in the old almanacs was probably more important than it appears in this age: it was an important part of farm equipment.

The farm superstitions about the moon are not something of the distant past, for some of them still persist. We all know that the expression "loony" comes from the superstition that you get that way from sleeping beneath lunar light; being "touched in the head" also came from the idea of being "touched by moonlight." And although in this age it seems like nonsense, few country mothers will today let their children sleep with the full moon shining on them. It is fantastic how such tales live on, but reading from an 1854 newspaper I find that "John Swift of Kent awoke after sleeping in the light of the full moon, with his face entirely swollen and his eyes blackened." And the *Scientific American* from the same year tells about "a person who threw a catch of fish in his wagon without bothering to cover them from the rays of the full moon. When he arrived at home four hours later, the fish were so green and putrefied that he had to throw them away." It is odd how anything in print has such a profound impact of "truth" upon the average reader.

Jimmy's job of demolition became simpler at ten o'clock, when a full moon rose over the horizon and made the night seem like day. He says a full moon hurts his eyes and makes him squint, and I cannot tell whether he is giving me some of his New England humor or telling the truth.

No one, I understand, has solved the riddle of why the moon looks bigger when it comes over the horizon than when it is overhead. This has been worrying mankind for centuries. If you take a camera shot of the moon near the horizon, it will look like a star instead of the moon, but look at it on the scene and the effect of size is almost overwhelming. It was once thought the illusion was caused by comparison of the moon to objects such as trees and houses along the horizon; but you get the same effect when the moon rises over an open sea.

My explanation of the illusion would lean toward color. The sun and moon are seen through a longitudinal mass of terrestrial dust, when close to the horizon, making them appear red; and although few people take it into consideration, color (particularly red) has definite motion effect. According to the early painters, blue recedes, yellow is motionless and red "comes toward you." By this rule, a room painted blue or bluish will appear larger because its walls will seem to go away from you. The same room painted in shades of red will appear smaller because its walls will "approach" you. The reverse applies to dress; a woman with a blue gown will look smaller, while the one with a red gown will "grow larger" as you look at her. So I do believe that the acceptance of the moon as being blue-white in our mind's eye is shocked by the appearance of a red moon, and color psychology takes over, distorting our night vision.

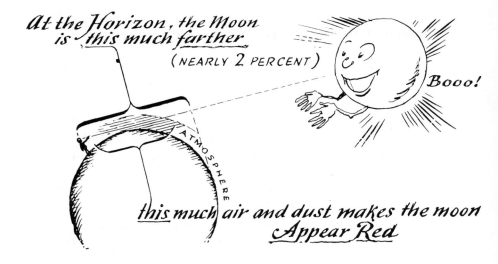

At the Horizon, the Moon is this much farther (NEARLY 2 PERCENT)

Booo!

ATMOSPHERE

this much air and dust makes the moon Appear Red

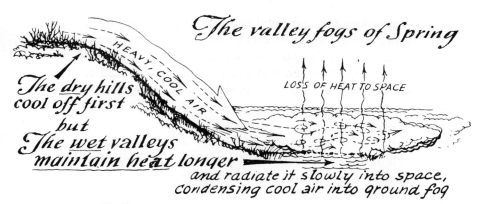

The valley fogs of Spring

HEAVY COOL AIR

The dry hills cool off first

but

The wet valleys maintain heat longer

LOSS OF HEAT TO SPACE

and radiate it slowly into space, condensing cool air into ground fog

Most of the winter's frost has left the ground by now, and much of the moisture that a month ago was locked in the landscape now hangs in pools of mist and fog above the scattered patches of snow in the valley. There is very little wind to carry off nocturnal fogs, and the winter sun is still too low in the heavens to disperse it before mid-morning, so the farms in the valley find April a drab and wet month, with poor visibility and constant threat of late frosts. Descending from the hills, the cold air, which is heavier than warm air, flows by gravity down into the low-lands and settles there in pools that from an airplane (and even from this elevation at Weather Hill) look exactly like little lakes.

At night when the ground radiates, or loses its heat to space, the pools of heavier air that flow from the surrounding hills build up into masses of radiation fog that cover five or ten square miles at a time. Frequently when you are motoring at night and you ascend a hill and emerge from the fog or mist, the effect is like coming up to the surface of a sea.

I am certain that living in a valley is damper and less healthy than living in the circulating air of hills, and I have often wondered why all the early villages were nestled in between hills rather than near the tops of them. I suppose the reason is because towns were always built on waterways before the time of serviceable roads, when the rivers and streams were the only means for the transportation of lumber. Furthermore, towns usually built up around water-powered mills, which were necessarily in valleys.

The farms that were built high in the New England hills seemed to specialize in maple sugar, and several of the early sugar farmers lived to be well over a hundred years old, which in those days of short life was most unusual. The story got around and the legend was that maple sugar contributed to their long life. Now I have often wondered if living in the hills, in the high and dry air, had anything to do with the long life of those sugarmen. I feel sure that living in the damp valleys had much to do with the pitifully young ages of the early death rate.

I suppose the short life span of those days of dangerous childbirth, disease, and overwork explains why the people were so conscious of death. Almost as revealing as histories of what New England people did are some of the old inscriptions on gravestones, telling the manner in which they died. One in Cold Springs Harbor, Long Island, describes how the deceased was struck by the tiller of his boat while going through the Hell Gate whirlpools. Another says, "The little hero that lies here, was conquered by the diarrhea."

One of the tenants of Weather Hill had collected odd epitaphs, as was once the custom; and copied in the back of an old book that I found here were about a hundred of them. Here are a few.

This corpse is Phebe Thorps.

Here lies John Lowe, a firm believer in the Lord, the M. E. Church and Jeffersonian Democracy.

Here lies the body of Samuel Proctor
Who lived and died without a doctor.

Here lies the body of Farmer Jonathan Bull who was killed by one.

This is maple-sugaring time and although these Connecticut hills grow very little sugar in comparison to what they did a hundred years ago, there is much talk about the sugar business north and west of here. A batch of old newspapers that came with the house have made pleasant reading these cool nights; in gathering local lore, I find that maple sugar was very much in the news. One item tells about the sugar industry in nearby Otsego County. Rents in the early days were usually paid in produce such as wheat, lumber, potash or sugar; in that one year the leader of a small colony near Cooperstown received sixty thousand pounds of maple syrup in rentals. I wondered what a landowner would do with thirty tons of maple syrup, but the account continued to tell how the entire amount was taken to New York by wagon and refined into loaves of sugar. Half of the loaves were sold in New York and the other half taken back by the same wagon.

Knowing what roads were in those days, I cannot conceive how such a journey by wagon to refine your product would not eat up all the profits. The weather must have been a most important item, particularly during snow time. When a farmer had to pay his bills by the results of the weather and deliver them in spite of the weather, I can see why the old almanacs with their forecasts were the *Wall Street Journals* of their day. If a trip to New York took three days or three weeks according to the weather, such information was more than just bedtime reading.

This is the month that the fishing-tackle companies send out their advertising pamphlets. If the fish this summer bite as well on worms as they have for this winter's ice-fishers, I shall be content to use nightwalkers. But for the real pleasure of fishing, which is not necessarily catching fish, I'll take casting. When you can place a plug or a fly exactly where you want it, alongside some likely rock or stump, even though there isn't a fish there at all, you always catch one in your mind's eye and every cast is a success. I recall seeing newspaper photographs of Herbert Hoover in fishing garb and always feeling that his fishing consisted mainly of posing with rod in hand, until I read his words, "to go fishing is a chance to wash one's self with pure air, with the rush of the brook, or with the shimmer of the sun on blue water. It brings meekness and inspiration from the decency of nature, charity toward tackle makers, patience toward fish, a mockery of profits and egos, a quieting of hate, a rejoicing that you do not have to decide a darn thing until next week. And it is discipline in equality of men—for all men are equal before fish." I wonder why politicians say things like that after getting elected and never think to do so in their campaign speeches.

Tree RECOGNITION *by Action*

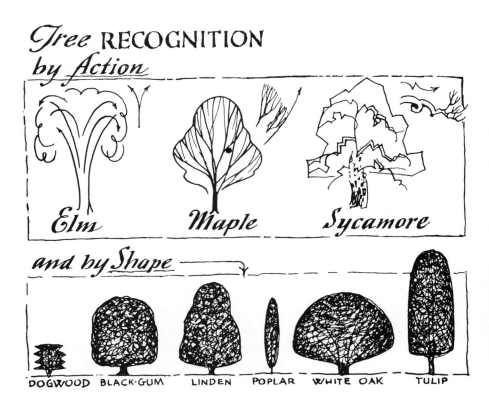

Elm Maple Sycamore

and by Shape

DOGWOOD BLACK-GUM LINDEN POPLAR WHITE OAK TULIP

This is the time of the year that the first buds appear, usually with the willows and swamp trees taking on a tinge of yellow-green. I want to do a few sketches of trees while they are still leafless; it is difficult to paint trees in foliage without knowing what goes on beneath the leaves, so I have promised myself a week of sketching to catch up on my tree anatomy. Just as I think of clouds as slow explosions of white, I find the frozen action of tree-growth typical of each kind of tree and very helpful in sketching it. The elm, for example, always reminds me of a skyrocket, for it shoots straight upward and then bursts out fanwise and ends in tiny "explosions" of falling leaves. The sycamore is a Javanese dancer to me, for its trunks go out boldly like a dancer's arms and then twist at the wrist into all sorts of weird contortions, as the drawing shows. If you are not familiar with the sycamore, it is the tree "with the wall-paper that is old and flaking off," like plaster showing through.

A hundred years ago all children could call off the name of every tree as they walked through the woods, but now they know few. When I was a youngster we had a game of calling out the names of automobiles as they went past, but now all automobiles look alike except for the colors. I think the tree-guessing game might come back again so here's a starter from my own observation.

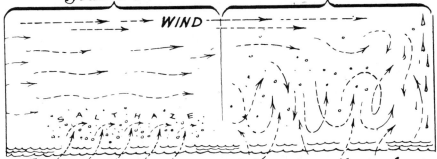

Why visibility at sea is often best before Rain

Stable air   *Unstable air*

WIND

SALT HAZE

Water with salt haze rising above its surface

Third Week of April

THE DULL DRABNESS of April persists, with poor visibility and frequent soft showers. Poor visibility is so often the sign of impending rain, yet this rule is sometimes reversed near the seashore. I have often heard an old salt say, "Look how near that ship on the horizon appears; it will certainly rain tomorrow." And there is a New England saying, "When the hills loom green and clear, that's the time a shower's near." I have never read any scientific references to that folklore, but my explanation would be that the unstableness of prestorm air tends to mix and carry upward and away the quantities of salt haze that seaside air is usually rich with. And properly mixed air is clear.

I never realized how rich with salt the coastal atmosphere is until it was called to my attention that the whitening of my chimney bricks was caused by salt in the air. Minute salt crystals are placed in the air by the evaporation of wave droplets within the atmosphere. So prolific is the formation of salt in the air that despite the removal of it by rainfall, there are hundreds of thousands of particles in each cubic inch of air up to several miles' altitude. These tiny invisible crystals are largely responsible for the blue color within the atmosphere, and the reason why the ocean sky often is bluer than the sky over land.

Yesterday I went to the town of Warren, where I heard an old barn is being torn down. I am in the market for seasoned chestnut wood to use in the making of frames for my paintings. Another artist found some fine old chestnut in a nearby tobacco barn that is still being used. He made a deal with the farmer to take what he needed for the paneling of a room with the condition that he would replace the old wood with new. The barn is a sort of landmark now, for half of it is covered with new white pine. The farmer thought he was getting the best of the deal, but my guess is that the new wood will last only five years before it rots. The old chestnut, which looked decayed on the outside, was actually so hard that the carpenter's electric saw smoked hotly when he cut it down to panel proportions.

The Warren barn is being torn down for a group of summer cottages, and while I was there, I thought I'd look them over. The builder mistook me for a prospective buyer and tried his best to sell me a house. It was interesting to note that modern home sales talk centers on convenience and cost with never a thought toward permanence. The reason, of course, is simple: permanence is almost a lost value in modern building. A hundred years ago, houses were built for your children and their children's children just as much as for you. Not now. I suppose the uncertainty of this atomic age makes day-to-day living more and more important.

The house I looked at was built on cinder blocks, ignoring a beautiful old barn foundation that was only twenty feet away. The builder noticed that my interest was centered on the old wall and he quickly said, "Don't worry about that—we are going to bulldoze that under. You'll never know it was there." What a pity that some people avoid anything associated with age.

Inside, however, the builder had done what he thought might attract the antique lover. He had hacked the new wood of the exposed beams to make them look hand-hewn. I wonder what the builder of Weather Hill would have thought of that, if he could have been there with me. I would have been ashamed for such modern misunderstanding.

Carl Sandburg has said that when men forget what they have done and where they came from, they have lost the foundation for going forward. It is a serious thing that so many of us have lost the ability to look backward intelligently, and that we think the only kind of progress concerns looking forward. The old ways have so much to offer besides age, but age, which is repulsive to the times we live in, is all some see in them. There is a sign on a nearby antique shop that reads WE BUY JUNK AND SELL ANTIQUES. It is very funny but it is also very sad.

This morning when I went for my daily walk to the lake, and while my dog Nimbo busied himself with a muskrat scent along the shore, I had time to sit and watch the actions of morning air. The sun had not yet eaten through the haze, and there was no heat circulation above the lake; the water was glassy with smoothness. But within a minute, the sun broke through and the quiet of the water was immediately shaken into action. It was as though a global light switch had turned on some invisible fan. It is all very well to read in meteorological textbooks how "the sun is the machine that operates the weather and circulates air," but those are just meaningless words compared to actually watching it happen. Within another minute after the sun had broken through, the lake had a complete pattern of corduroy ripples and all the leaves of the trees were in motion.

I recall hearing tales of how the first flyers who flew the low-powered boxlike biplanes always flew in the morning before the sun was well up in the heavens. In that way, they could avoid the daytime mixing of atmosphere and the circulation of gusts and vertical currents. After watching the sun's effect on the air above the lake, I can see what they meant.

Another thing about early flying that impressed me was discovering that cold air is easier to fly in; at least, you go slower because it is denser and harder to "push through." When I learned to fly, we always practiced take-offs and landings in the evening, when the sun was down. This avoided the bumpiness of midday air and also made landings slower. Actually you land about five to ten miles an hour faster on a hot day than you do on a cool day. Speed records are usually made over the heat of the desert during the middle of the day. At that time, much more speed is attained by bulleting through the warmer, thinner atmosphere.

As I look across the valley and see the tapestry of landscape and farms on the opposite hills, the shadows of clouds seem always to be present, giving added life to the pattern. When you can see well-defined cloud shadows, you are seeing downdraft machines at work, promoting thermals and aiding in the circulation of the air. They are like big spoons stirring up movement in the fluid atmosphere.

It is interesting how the warmed earth sends up thermals to create a cloud, which reflects back a portion of sun heat and cools the earth below. And all the while the invisible up and down winds of atmospheric global air conditioning are working to keep the sky circulated and clear.

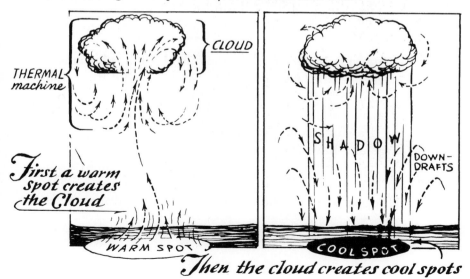

THERMAL machine

CLOUD

First a warm spot creates the Cloud

WARM SPOT

SHADOW

DOWN-DRAFTS

COOL SPOT

Then the cloud creates cool spots

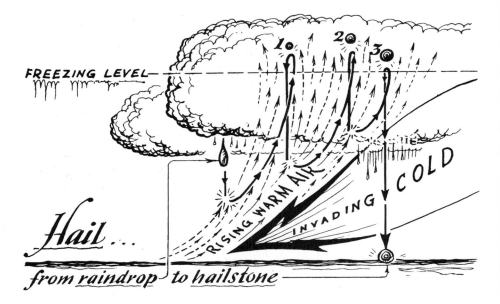

FREEZING LEVEL

1. 2. 3.

RISING WARM AIR

INVADING COLD

Hail ...

from raindrop to hailstone

**Last
Week
of
April**

IT IS ODD how we remember the accidents, the bad news and the untimely events, and so easily forget the rest. This week started with an early thunderstorm, and the occasion started a trigger of memory that recalled the same thing happening for many years back. A good day or a fine sunset fills your moment with pleasure without recalling the past. The country folk take sunshine for granted, but unusual weather always revives memories of "years ago when it was much worse."

The thundershower was accompanied by hail, which identified the weather change as a fast-moving cold front that "snowplowed" the warmer air into the frigid world that approaches the stratosphere, as shown by the dotted arrows in the drawing above. Not many stones fell, but they were as large as I have ever seen, and I felt called upon to slice one in half to prove what I had read so often in the weather books. I used a two-edged razor and a magnifying glass to find it quite true that there were layers—three distinct lines around the center drop. That proved that the large raindrop had taken three trips into the freezing zone, booted by the hurricane updraft of the cold front, and had finally become heavy enough to resist it and fall to my doorstep as hail.

It was the peal of thunder that made me recall the past thundershowers of very early spring. There is something that isn't frightening at all about early thunder, because it welcomes the new season. It is rather like the difference between war guns and welcome guns.

Earl Gann is cutting down the poison ivy around the place before it blossoms. I heard of several recent hospital cases of ivy poisoning and almost shudder when I think of the children who walk barefoot in the stuff. Why was poison ivy put into the world? Birds and animals eat poison-ivy berries without ill effects, so I probably have my answer right there. Perhaps man and the condition of his skin is not as important in the scheme of things as we suppose. Earl told me that he is immune, however, and to prove it he rubbed his bare arms with a handful of the roots and finished off like a showman by munching them and swallowing the juice. "An old Choctaw Indian showed me how to do that," he said, "and I haven't had ivy poisoning since. Used to have it something awful as a child." I would have rather seen him swallow broken glass. I certainly hope Earl and the Choctaw Indian are right; I have heard of people who spent their summer taking food through a hospital tube after doing the same thing.

Earl, who has a penchant for braving ivy and all the elements of nature, intended to work right through the hail and shower, but a particularly loud thunderclap sent him meekly indoors and away from his metal scythe.

I have often wondered why thunder seems to echo just as long on the open plains as it does in mountainous regions. But a scientific friend picked up an erroneous reference I had made to the echoing of thunder. He explained to me that *thunder does not echo at all*. The prolonged rumbling is caused by the length and irregularity of the lightning flash. A gun makes one solid "bang" because the explosion comes from one place—within the gun. But a lightning explosion occurs at many different distances from you, sometimes from a two-mile-long and very irregular flash. As sound travels comparatively slowly, this lengthy explosion reaches your ears as a prolonged rumble because it is coming from a variety of different places. Frequently, the lightning flash will arc overhead, and although the resulting "bang" will be coming from different places, it all reaches you at the same time: that effect, which is known as a "thunderclap," is one loud explosion instead of the usual rumbling.

Why some thunder rumbles and some "claps"

3 SEC.

1 SEC.

6 SEC.

RUMBLING THUNDER

THIS·EXPLOSION·REACHES
YOU·AT·DIFFERENT·INTERVALS

1 SEC.   1 SEC.   1 SEC.

THUNDERCLAP

THIS·EXPLOSION·REACHES
YOU·ALL·AT·ONE·INSTANT

Weather tends to move 5 to 6 hundred miles a day, Eastward (FASTEST·IN·WINTER)

WEATHER MAP

W / E

This storm— MIGHT·BE·EXPECTED·HERE) TOMORROW

"Yellow streaks in sunset sky, wind and day-long rain is nigh!"

First mentioned by Jesus Christ (Matthew 16), the sunset sign is probably the best known of all old-time weatherlore. Tonight the sunset sky was pale and yellow, streaking off into gray. It shall indeed rain tomorrow.

The truth in this saying lies in the fact that most of our weather tends to move from west to east, about five hundred miles a day: the western sky is therefore atmosphere which will reach you tomorrow. In other words, the setting sun is always shining through weather to come. If that sky is clear, the sun's reflection against it will be clear and the sky will easily reflect the redness of the sun; but if that sky is wet and stormy, the sun's reflection will be wan and the sky will glow in a pale manner.

Most people mistake "red sky" for red sun and thereby lose the whole point of the prediction. The sun at sunset sinks through concentrated terrestrial dust and is therefore always red. What the folklore refers to is the sky surrounding the sun, not the sun itself.

This week was marked by my ascent of Great Mountain. Without ropes or crampons and equipped with no more than a chocolate bar for myself and some dog biscuits for Nimbo, we made the trip feeling like real adventurers. When you stop to think that only a hundred years ago there were no public roads other than dirt trails and a few toll turnpikes, travelers must frequently have had to make such shortcuts over mountains. There were places where the sun did not reach, where there was still snow and ice, so the going was slow and muddy.

According to New England standards, anything higher than a thousand feet is a mountain, and Great Mountain is 1074 feet. Whatever it lacks by way of height, however, it makes up for in its amazing steepness of slope. Loosened rocks as big as ferryboats are piled in profusion, looking even bigger as they rest on trees torn from their roots, some exposing shattered trunks with bursts of twenty-foot splinters. The scene gives the impression of a gigantic landslide frozen in action. As quiet as it is, everything still seems to be hurtling. This is the sort of sight that inspired those artists of the Hudson River School, whose paintings are now criticized for being too imaginative and for presenting a too exalted conception of the American scene. One of those critics should have climbed Great Mountain with me.

As I neared the top, I became aware of a change in vegetation. At home, this first week of May, the white sumac has sprouted; I remembered this because I had instructed Earl Gann to scythe down all the poisonous white sumac and leave the nonpoisonous red sumac. But here on top of the mountain, the sumacs had not yet begun to sprout. Then I remembered hearing from a hilltop farmer that things bloom later at higher altitudes. The rule of thumb, I believe, is two weeks for every thousand feet.

How often have I gone to the country to find the trees a week or two "behind time" in foliage. I always presumed this to be the result of country air being colder than that of city areas, but higher elevation must have much to do with it.

Looking down at the carpet of farms and the fat fingers of water that make up Candlewood Lake, the world looked green and lush. Far off I could see tiny automobiles moving very slowly along the highway: a rise of dust seemed to stay with a "motionless" tractor that was changing a pasture from green to brown. Distance has a slowing-up effect; like the vapor-trailed jet planes that seem to be crawling slowly in the sky, these things were traveling faster than they appeared.

Emerson often spoke about how, to one looking down from a height, time in the valley seemed slower. As I looked at the scene, I recalled his words: "The day, immeasurably long, sleeps over the broad hills and warm wide fields." High above, in the sky, were long feathery streaks of cirrus clouds. These "mares' tails" too seemed motionless, although they were probably scratching the ceiling of weather at some two hundred miles an hour. It is good to see things from a great distance and so to slow them up. It makes life seem longer and assures you that there still is time for the things you want to do before it is too late.

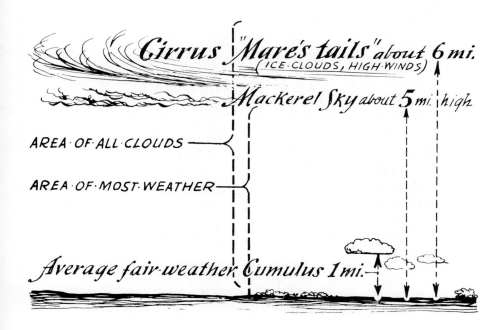

*Timbers all hewed and
numbered and laid:
Cider's a'poured and biscuits
are made...*

OLD·BARN-RAISING·SONG

Second Week of May

JIMMY came by to finish piling up the old barn beams. The two roof shoulders were thirty feet long with adze marks as sharp and definite as if they had been done yesterday, and "raising-numbers" in Roman numerals matching all joints.

The removal of the barn brought to view several apple trees that had been chewed noticeably by deer. "Those trees haven't bore fruit much to speak of," said Jimmy, "but that chewing might spur up a better crop." Not knowing what he meant, I pursued the subject and learned that farmers believe partial girdling, or "ringing," as Jimmy called it, is a good remedy for a tree that yields too little fruit. Possibly the shock to the health of a tree by a trunk wound, and its effort to fight back and recover, does spur the yield of fruit: perhaps it is just superstition. But I found in my almanac library an old proverb, "A barren apple tree doth grow better fruit if torn by blow," which implies that trees strained or split by the wind tend to yield more and better fruit. It was a New England custom to "pepper old fruit trees," Jimmy tells me, and farmers around here used to blast away with a shotgun at close range to make an old tree bear again. I found the same thing mentioned in the customs and superstitions of European farm folk, who still "shoot barren trees."

From where the barn was, there is now a view covering a fine stretch of countryside. The occasional drone of a truck as it moves beetle-fashion across the landscape makes me all too aware of Route 7 and the promise of streets and roads that will some day blot out this scene forever. Instead of being only glad that I am still able to behold this farm view, I also have a great sorrow for those who will be deprived of it. Worse still, they will be just as content without it.

Perhaps it is one of this week's letters that gives me a philosophic moodiness. It was a reply from an editor of a farm magazine to which I had submitted an article about early American barns. "I'm sorry," it read, "but at the present time this magazine and the American farmer is only interested in practical up-to-date structures having to do with progressive agriculture, and not with history." I know full well that the ancient hand-hewn barn would be useless on any farm of today, but the thought that today's farmer fails so to recognize the spiritual and architectural heritage left him by those who molded the farms is disheartening.

The farm boy of the distant tomorrow, I suppose, will never know the joy of a swimming hole, the fun of a barn-raising or a night in the hayloft. He won't even be able to read about it in the farm magazines.

On my way to town I passed a farmhouse and barn that are in the process of being built. The barn is made of plastics and metal; it looks very much like a factory. The farmhouse is lacking in the architectural dignity that makes New England the delight that it has been for three hundred years. There is a flat roof and, whereas builders usually place a small ceremonial bough on the rooftree as soon as the rafters have been put in place, they have put there instead (even before the roofing has been completed) a television antenna!

I have often tried to define for myself the psychological difference between the architecture of today and yesterday. We pride ourselves with claim to "functional modern," yet the earliest buildings were extremely functional, for actual survival. The real difference, I do believe, was a difference in thinking. Our timesavers, our conveniences, and now our atomic bombs have made us less confident of the future; we think less far into the future and build only for today. Few people would buy a ranch house with an eye toward a future generation. The result is a house that will be gone in fifty or a hundred years. Today we buy homes and change them almost as we do our clothes.

Americana 1756   *Americana 1956*

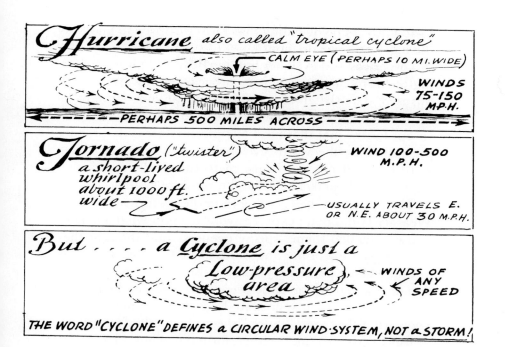

Hurricane, also called "tropical cyclone"

— CALM EYE (PERHAPS 10 MI. WIDE)

WINDS 75-150 M.P.H.

—— — PERHAPS 500 MILES ACROSS — — — ——

Tornado ("twister") — WIND 100-500 M.P.H.
a short-lived whirlpool about 1000 ft. wide —
——USUALLY TRAVELS E. OR N.E. ABOUT 30 M.P.H.

But . . . . a __Cyclone__ is just a __Low-pressure__ area — WINDS OF ANY SPEED

THE WORD "CYCLONE" DEFINES a CIRCULAR WIND-SYSTEM, NOT a STORM!

Third Week of May

IF YOU ARE ASKED to recall an exceptionally beautiful morning in your life, it will probably turn out to have been a morning in May. "May is a broom," says one of my almanacs, "of a bright-faced angel that sweeps the sky clean for the coming of summer." After the clouded overcast of April, May is noted for its blue-skied mornings. The *Clergyman's Almanac* of 1818 starts this month's page with, "How delightful is the countryside at this season when the sun rises in cloudless majesty," and it supports the phenomenon with a Biblical quotation on May: "And he shall be as the light of the morning, when the sun riseth, even a morning without clouds . . ." (2 Samuel 23:4).

As noted as May is for clear mornings, it also has some claim to fame for stormy afternoons, for May heads the list for tornado occurrences. It also heads the list for hail occurrences. Spring weather and the "merry month of May" are so accepted as being balmy that I was surprised to find May the hail-and-tornado month.

Tornadoes and cyclones and hurricanes are very confusing terms to the average person because they are so often misused. The sketch above should set anyone straight on the differences. The actual cyclone need not involve a storm except for the fact that most low-pressure areas do produce precipitation; the word "cyclone" comes from the Greek word for "coiled," and its use meteorologically means that the wind coils snakelike around a pressure system.

The hylas have been crying from the pasture across from Weather Hill. I don't expect anyone to know what a hyla is: I always called them "spring peepers" and thought they were frogs. One of my anecdotes has been concerning my youth, when I parked my Reo roadster under a full moon and near a marsh where the peepers were serenading. "Isn't it wonderful," I whispered to the girl beside me, "do you know what they are?" "Sure," she replied, "they're turtles."

But I wasn't so smart either, for today when I looked up my "frogs" in the nature library, I found they are really hylas, or tree toads named from the Greek word *hyle* for wood. They were the ancient symbol for spring, as mentioned by Aristophanes twenty-three hundred years ago.

When I moved into Weather Hill there were a number of bullfrogs in the old discarded spring behind the barns, probably doing their job of keeping the water clean, as they did a hundred and fifty years ago. Their voice at night was at the same time awesome and comforting, like the bay of an old watchdog. The men who came with the moving trucks were impressed by the croaking that started long before sundown. They suggested there was a good supper of frogs' legs to be had there. Only a city person would say such a thing. I would have been eating my slumber music for the whole summer!

This week I saw an old friend leave, one who traveled seventy-five thousand wonderful miles with me. My station wagon was traded in on a new one. How ridiculous to have sentiment toward a machine; yet I did. In these days we live a great part of our lives on the road, and you would think there would be more sentiment attached to one's automobile, foolish as it may seem. Yet we forget the old car quickly.

Frequently an antique-car collector will find a rare early model hiding away in a locked barn, and wonder why the owner did not get rid of it the way we do nowadays. The reasons, I daresay, were locked away against the world— fond moments of picnics, children who climbed over the cushioned seats, a kiss along some old road or just a feeling of great gratitude for the days and hours and years of travel that always ended up at home. There are still those who weep when the family car is traded in, and car salesmen who look on in amazement, not realizing that the tears are for an emblem and not machinery.

Spring skies are typically chaotic. The few clouds of May always look as though they are undecided whether to be fair-weather or rain-bearing. I have observed that a uniformity in clouds, whether it be in the anatomy of the cloud itself or in the overall pattern of clouds, is a sign of good weather. Clouds that are irregularly placed in the sky, or clouds that have the irregular appearance of shellbursts, are more apt to develop into rain machines. Good flat bottoms and oval tops on cumulus clouds seem to predict fair skies; tufted tops and raggy bottoms predict showers.

THE·APPEARANCE·OF·CUMULUS·CLOUDS·SUGGESTS·COMING WEATHER

OVAL TOP

FLAT·BOTTOM

TOWER TOPS

RAGGED BOTTOM

Regularly placed FAIR

Irregularly placed RAIN

a miniature STEAM FOG on the forge barn

steam fog in full scale... over water

COOL AIR

WARMTH

WATER RETAINS ITS HEAT

Last Week of May

MEMORIAL DAY WEEK has traditionally been a week of uncertain weather. The almanacs in my complete library note this time with such sayings as, "Now it is hot, now it is not," "Windy with showers," "The clouds are low."

The barometer has been jumpy and the weather raw; I believe things will clear by the holiday. I lit a fire in the forge-barn studio this morning and an hour later I looked out to see if all was well there. The whole roof was pouring white smoke and I lost no time in dashing out with a fire extinguisher. But my "smoke" turned out to be nothing but condensation clouds from the sun's heat on the ancient shingles, which were very cold and wet. This phenomenon, like the steam from a sprinkled sidewalk during summer, is called steam fog. I've often seen it during winter when a cold breeze blows across warm water, in which case it is often referred to as "sea smoke."

Attics are renowned for their ability to collect antiques. My stone wall runs a close second, and I wonder if other stone walls have the same trait. Because the walls were really just neatly piled discard from cleared fields, farmers often regarded them as good places to throw anything that was useless around the farm. I removed a part of my wall and found several handmade hinges, the remains of twenty old saws, discarded scythe blades and many broken medicine bottles of handmade glass. Stone walls are usually parallel lines of set stones with the round and odd-shaped rocks thrown in the middle; it is there in the middle that you will find the relics.

One of my favorite stories is about the city lady who wrote to Sears Roebuck and Company asking if they could supply her with a stone wall for her country home. But I guess it wasn't as funny as I thought, because today I see an advertisement in the Newtown *Bee* offering a stone wall for sale.

One of the prizes from the wall was a silver thimble. Peeking from beneath the tarnish and weathering was the inscription *John Hancock*. I rushed in to do some research and found that most gentlemen of that day did sew, and they often owned their own thimbles. But the thrill of my great find was burst when I cleaned the thimble completely and found the full signature to be *John Hancock Insurance Company.*

I also found the broken tip of a broadax. I could tell it was a broadax because only one side of the cutting edge was beveled. Broadaxes were used more as planes, and not to cut things in two as most people think. You "felled" with an ax and "hewed" it smooth or square with a broadax.

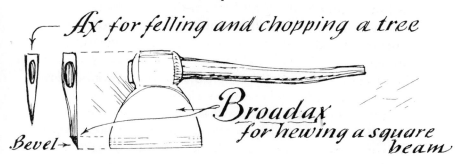

Ax for felling and chopping a tree

Bevel→

Broadax for hewing a square beam

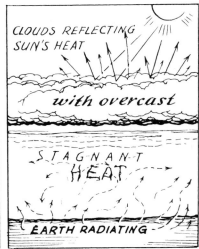

First Week of June

THIS WEEK has been clouded and warmer. It does not seem logical for a clouded day to be warm, but a covered sky produces less atmospheric circulation and the little warmth that radiates from the earth collects in stagnant pockets. On a sunshiny day you get heat directly from the sun and it is a dry warmth, but on a cloudy day you get a moist heat from the earth.

The drawing shows the clouds reflecting back some of the sun's heat (a factor we seldom think about). Eighty per cent of solar heat never reaches the earth, being reflected back into space by clouds, dust and other air particles. I raked and burned some of winter's leaves this morning, to flavor the morning for my breakfast, and the slow erratic ascent of smoke was a fine indication of the day's poor atmospheric circulation.

One may often forget the month, but that seldom occurs in June: no month makes you more aware of its character. Perhaps it is the long looking forward to summer weather, perhaps it is the lively interpretation that poets have given; but when June arrives, you are completely aware of it.

Late-spring rain seems always to be gentle; this first week of June has given the countryside three such caresses. I looked up June in an old almanac to see what the weather should have been doing two hundred years ago and found frequent use of the phrase "fine showers." I like that, and wish that the weather bureau would make use of it, it is so descriptive of spring rain, which is often like the laciest spray of a lawn sprinkler.

When the skies are dark and someone asks me if it is going to rain, my first calculation concerns the height of the clouds. If they are low, the chance of rain is greatest, but if the clouds are at five thousand feet or more (and do not tend to lower), you may expect no rain regardless of how dark they become. Spring rains are often light or "fine" because of the height of rain clouds; the rain falls so far through the warm air that by the time it reaches earth, each rain-drop has already begun to evaporate back into the atmosphere. The miracle of water droplets being born from the air and then returning to it silently is typical of the symphony of weather. The life cycle of rain can be likened to that of all living things; the secret of rain, like the secret of life, has still not been solved, even by the meteorologists. Only in philosophy and poetry, it seems, has the life cycle of rain been satisfactorily discussed. Consider Shelley, who in 1820 was an accurate meteorologist when he wrote:

> *I am the daughter of Earth and Water,*
> *And the nursling of the Sky:*
> *I pass through the pores of the ocean and shores;*
> *I change, but I cannot die.*
> *For after the rain, when with never a stain*
> *The pavilion of heaven is bare,*
> *And the winds and sunbeams with their convex gleams*
> *Build up the blue dome of air,*
> *I silently laugh at my own cenotaph,*
> *And out of the caverns of rain,*

Like a child from the womb, like a ghost from the tomb,
I arise, and unbuild it again.

How perfectly has Shelley pictured moisture passing from
its liquid state in the sea to a gaseous state in the atmosphere.
Then at a height it bursts back into liquid again as cloud
droplets: finally it disappears into the atmosphere again as
gas. Moisture, as Shelley has put it, changes but never dies.
Even one who dislikes poetry must salute words like those.

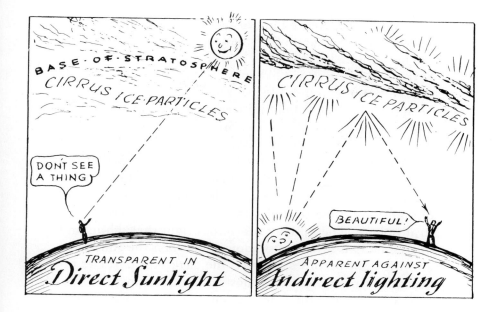

THIS WEEK marks the earliest sunrise of the year. The birds began chattering at my window at the minute of sunrise, a few minutes after four in the morning. I rose to pull the drapes and give myself a few hours' more sleep, and was amazed at the crimson sky and blinding red sun. The barns in the valley were lit; I suppose the farmers were already up. They say that when a New England farmer has a holiday, he still gets up at daybreak to get in his full day of loafing.

Benjamin Franklin, who always enjoyed working late into the night and sleeping soundly into the morning, was once wakened at six in the morning by the rising sun. In one of his letters he wrote: ". . . still thinking it something extraordinary that the sun should rise so early, I looked into the almanac, where I found it to be the hour given for his rising on that day. I say it is impossible that so sensible a people should have lived so long by the smoky, unwholesome, and enormously expensive light of candles, if they might have known, that they might have had as much pure light of the sun for nothing."

It is surprising to one like myself who sees so few sunrises that they are so much like sunsets in appearance. I have been painting duck-shooting scenes for so long without realizing my early-morning skies might well have been sunset skies. The greatest difference is in the presence of mist on the earth in the morning, which reflects a blue color upward and produces a violet shade which is seldom seen at dusk.

At sunrise and sunset we are able to behold the fine layer of transparent ice particles that hover at the base of the stratosphere. The midday sun shines right through it, and like Peter Pan it has no shadow. But when the sun is low and the light becomes indirect, the cirroform particles reflect the crimson light in a most brilliant manner.

Few people use the word "treenware" for woodenware; still fewer know that the word comes from the early word "treen," or plural for "trees." But when farmer Wanzer stopped by for a chat and referred to my collection of wooden tools and kitchen utensils as treenware, I was delighted.

There were several wooden tools that I had not yet identified: one was a paddlelike instrument of honey-colored maple which I had guessed to be a butter paddle. "A fine bed-patter you have there," remarked Wanzer. "I haven't seen one of those since childhood days." And so a small mystery was solved. Feather mattresses, he explained, needed a great deal of patting and flattening, and early New England households always had one of these wooden bed-patters on hand to do the job.

a Connecticut
Bed-patter

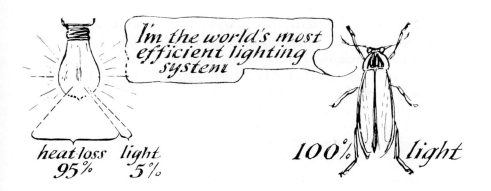

I'm the world's most efficient lighting system

heat-loss 95%   light 5%

100%   light

THE WEATHER has settled to a comfortably warm quietness. The steady, high barometer readings confirm that we are within a large area of high pressure. Nights are. almost like stage sets and I know what the poets mean when they refer to a night in June. I saw the first fireflies last night, many hundreds of them blinking in the meadow against the black backdrop of the woods behind. Fireflies do not flash in strong light, and oddly enough, they will not flash in complete darkness. Only in dusk do you see their light.

No one has solved the riddle of the firefly's light, but if man could duplicate it he would be able to produce illumination without heat loss. Electric light bulbs lose about ninety-five per cent of their energy in heat, with only three to ten per cent producing the light.

This week I heard a new twist to an old superstition—one that bears investigation. With the aid of a local farm-carpenter, I put up a carport shed and thought it fitting to tack up a small tree or bush on the new roof, "for luck." To carry out the ceremony I also brought out a jug of cider to "wet the bush," as the custom dictates, and my friend and I knocked off a few moments to drink and chat. He referred to the ceremonial tree as a "fire-bush" and he said it "guarded the new roof against catching fire." I'd never heard this one before, but in one of my almanacs I did find

109

reference to a "fire-bush." It was a broomlike bush kept handy to whack out fires around the farm.

"Let every housekeeper keep a fire-bush 6 or 8 feet long," it reads, "with good green tops, to whip out a fire at its first start."

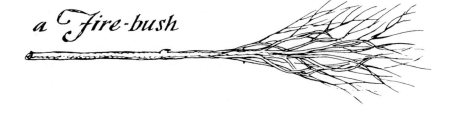

a Fire-bush

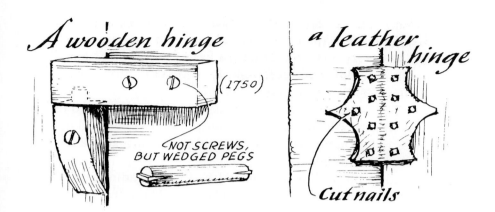

A wooden hinge (1750)

NOT SCREWS,
BUT WEDGED PEGS

a leather hinge

Cut nails

THE FIRST WEEK of summer is done with, and all the countryside seems aware of the new season. Even the clouds, which are higher in summer, seem already different.

It is often said that down on the farm they never throw anything away. Today I learned why. I broke the Sabbath by doing a little fixing around the place, and in trying to bend an ancient pantry door hinge, I broke it. The stores being closed, I decided to fashion a leather hinge. An old belt of mine which Mr. Miller had fished out of a trash pile proved the New England adage that "there's a use for anything if you wait long enough."

Cowhide hinges and wooden hinges were the only kinds found in the first houses of America. Handmade iron strap hinges were added later, but because of the king's tax on metal hardware, most barn doors swung on leather or wood hinges until the end of the eighteenth century.

I like to think my old belt will swing my pantry door for years. It is odd what great satisfaction one gets from improvising or designing something useful, no matter how trivial.

A boatbuilder in search of seasoned wood came by during the week. I suppose through Jimmy and the farmers in the valley word had gone around that I had taken down a barn and that there were several pieces of seasoned oak to be had. The wood, however, was not exactly what he was looking for, but the occasion called for a pleasant chat and a coffee break. I learned that the man is not a professional boatbuilder but that he has always wanted to build a boat for himself, using the best of materials, and without hurrying. The best oak he could buy, he told me, had warped or split while the boat was still in construction. So he had decided to look to the old barns around the vicinity for better-seasoned material.

Oddly enough, just last night I had been reading reports of how the early farmers of England built the framework for their barns from old boats. This seemed to be the only way they could get good seasoned oak for building, because the best wood was reserved for the navy. Royal scouts worked daily marking every suitable oak, making it navy property by the king's mark. I understand that up until a few years ago there were still a few old trees in New England bearing the "king's broad arrow."

One of the strangest stories has just come to light regarding the custom of British farmers to buy the timbers from old sailing craft. It seems that the *Mayflower* was sold in England in 1624 by permission of the British Admiralty; it brought about five hundred dollars. The wood went to a Buckingham farmer named William Russell, for building his barn. There it stands now, seasoned by the salt of the famous voyage, a building made entirely from the history-making ship *Mayflower*.

The barn that was the "Mayflower"

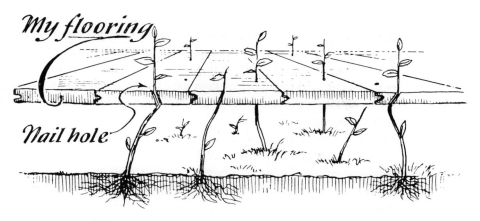

My flooring

Nail hole

For little more than rural conversation, I asked farmer Wanzer how his crops were coming, and he said something that set me to thought. "The clouds," he said, "have held up growing. Like the Bible says, in the beginning things need light." And how right farmer Wanzer was, for I looked it up in my farm book and find that it is the full cycle of daylight that actually produces budding. Strawberries will not flower, I learned, when the day length is from ten to eleven hours long. They produce most when the day length is fourteen to fifteen hours long.

I have never ceased to be amazed at the need for light that living plants have, and the manner in which they seek the sun. Is it a mechanical movement or is it an evidence of spirit that causes plants to lean in the direction of the sun? This week has given me an experience that makes me think plants may have a sort of mentality in that direction.

Recently in making a studio for painting, I moved the old forge barn to a clearing where there were a few silverweeds growing. Above the ground about two feet I built a flooring made from the old seasoned pine boards that once covered the large barn. Now in this rough flooring, there are about fifty old nail holes, probably as big around as the thin lead used in mechanical pencils. Yet through every one of these small holes, I now find a silverweed plant growing, sprouting through the floor and up into the room.

To the plants growing in the blackness below, the flooring above was probably like a night sky, and the fifty faint dots of light like stars. For a plant to pick out so faint a speck of light and to direct its growth exactly at the nearest one seems to indicate intent, ability, and at least some sort of intelligence.

The plants seemed to have the spirit of accomplishment in the way they grew straight and green into my room. I actually felt guilty of cruelty when I ripped them up. I shall never look at the night sky without thinking of my studio floor and the way those silverweed sprouts must have contemplated the starlike specks of light above them.

This was my first Fourth of July without seeing fireworks: Connecticut has joined the rest of the states that have outlawed them. I contributed something to the Fourth, however, by calling Earl 'Gann and asking him to do some trapshooting with me. The stores around here do not seem to carry clay pigeons but I used a pair of my old shoes. I now own ventilated oxfords, slightly heavier from buckshot, but still wearable. I am sure the sound carried across the valley and throughout the countryside, for as soon as we began shooting, other shots sounded from here and there. By noon, it seemed that everyone in the area was doing the same thing. There are so many gun enthusiasts in America who limit themselves to killing game, I wonder why there are not more rifle ranges and skeet clubs that can be used all year round. Guns are just as noisy as firecrackers; handled rightly they are safer. Next year I shall have a trap-shooting party on the Fourth of July: who knows, perhaps it will catch on and become the holiday custom.

Earl brought his own gun but it is dented near the muzzle, and a hole has been worn completely through; I asked him not to shoot it but he insisted. I was surprised to see a puff of smoke coming from the hole each time he shot. He has the fantastic idea that the "vent hole" improves the pattern of his gun, and he prefers it to my favorite Francotte.

The nostalgia of my early glorious Fourths make me regret the passing of fireworks. Square dances, pie suppers and bingo parties cannot reflect the spirit of the holiday as well as one bunch of four-inch salutes. I never smell gunpowder or the pulpy odor of burning cardboard without thinking of those wonderful Fourths of July.

New Jersey has passed a bill making firecrackers legal by permit for the purpose of scaring birds away from cornfields. The method used is to hang long ropes from tripods with firecrackers about eight inches apart, their fuses stuck through the strands of rope. When the rope is lit to smolder from the bottom, the firecrackers go off at intervals.

I haven't seen a good scarecrow in years. They disappeared when farmers began dangling wartime aluminum scrap to scare the birds. Rabbits seem to be the menace now, perhaps because farmers have fewer dogs than they used to. A farmer in the valley has some cowbells rigged up in his vegetable garden with a wire extending to a hook near his refrigerator in the kitchen. Every time he opens his refrigerator he remembers to pull the wire, which scares the rabbits away even on the darkest night. The old-fashioned scarecrow was part of our rural scene. Even if it wasn't very effective, it was an outlet for a man to show his sense of humor. Whenever I saw a scarecrow done up in an old bonnet and an apron I just knew that the farmer was poking fun at his wife, who probably "aimed" to set up another scarecrow in her own kitchen garden, with boots and bandana, and poke fun right back at him. There seemed to be a sort of rural culture connected with scarecrow designing. A psychologist could probably tell you a lot about a farmer by analyzing his scarecrow.

115

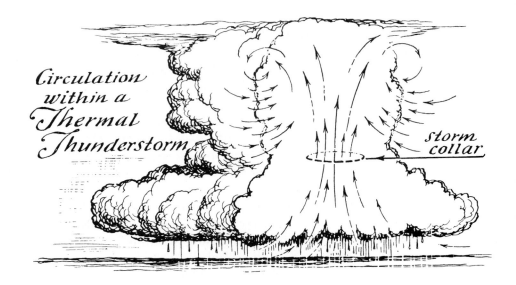

Circulation within a Thermal Thunderstorm

storm collar

Second Week of July

THIS has been a week of surprise showers. Not storms caused by the invasion of a new air mass, but little storms that grew by themselves. Most summer thermals burst into cumulus clouds which disappear back into the circulation of summer skies before they can reach thunderhead proportions. But now and then a cumulus cloud is fed with such violent updrafts that it grows into a vaporous giant. Then, with good-weather machinery that has gone out of control, a thermal thunderstorm is born.

Toward the end of any summer day you may see these bad boys of the heavens sulking and brooding in the purple distance along the horizon. Those that were big enough to withstand the cloud-melting effect of sundown will continue into the dark like quarrelsome children who won't go to bed, disturbing the summer night with so-called heat lighting. Heat lightning is no more than the flashing of eastbound storms that will never reach you—scattered showers that are over the southern or eastern horizon.

If the words "scattered showers" were ruled out of meteorology, the weatherman would be at a loss; that phrase is often as close as he can get to a pinpoint prediction during

116

warm weather. A thermal thunderstorm can appear from no-where and start a two-mile-wide course in such an erratic path that an accurate prediction is out of the question. The more concentrated the storm, the more abrupt its boundary edges.

My neighbor Martha Sawyers phoned me during the week to get my opinion on the weather for her outdoor bar-becue. The barometer was lowering and so were the dark cumulus clouds, so I predicted a thunderstorm. When the rain hit, I felt proud of myself to the extent even of forget-ting about my newly planted late grass seed, which washed away. But Martha, who·lives not more than three miles away, swears that not even a drop of rain fell there. I know how the weatherman must feel.

Concentrated summer showers used to have the respect of flyers, but today's airline pilots treat them as a bus driver re-gards bumps along the road. On a long flight the airliner will lift up over the storm, but on a short hop such storms are small enough for the plane to fly around. Because they are whirl-pools in the sea of summer air that move in a counterclock-wise manner (in the northern hemisphere), you fly past them to the right. If you try passing them toward the left, you risk running into a headwind; going to the right you will get the beneficial push of a tailwind.

Some day I shall invest in a good telescope to watch ther-mal-thunderstorm clouds. I recall seeing them while flying and I wonder if one may get the same thrill by watching them from land through a glass. Although thunderhead clouds appear to have no motion, at close range they are boiling. The false cirrus veil toward the top, which when viewed from a distance seems to float like mist, is really a foaming cloud; it is as if a thousand demons are shoveling snow out from its depths. The lightning charges from within the cloud, too weak to be observed from the ground, make an almost continuous flicker, giving the impression of fire.

Before one of this week's showers ended, a most unusual rainbow appeared, giving me much pleasure. More brilliant than any I had yet seen, this rainbow touched the ground exactly three hundred feet from my doorway. There is a clearing in the pasture where it ended, and its outlines were so distinct that you could determine between which patches of grass the colors were hovering. As I watched, a secondary bow appeared, about fifty feet above the first bow, but this one faded away as it approached the earth and did not "touch the ground." The main bow had its primary color of red, yellow, and blue going outward in that order, but the secondary bow had its colors reversed. In other words, one bow had its red on the outside of the arc and the other bow had its red on the inside. This phenomenon interested me so, and I was so entranced by the whole spectacle, that I did not think about walking over to where the rainbow was. Now that it is over, I wonder if the mirage would have continued to appear the same distance away, had I walked toward it. Never before had I supposed that a rainbow could be measured so closely. If it occurs again, I shall try not to be awed, and shall busy myself with research, or at least photograph it.

Remembering the fabled "pot of gold" at the end of the rainbow, I was tempted to search the pasture. Oddly enough, I had been seeking a site to do my "one good painting of the year," and had considered that same spot in the pasture. I shall be just that childish and superstitious, to choose that "end of the rainbow" site to set up my easel: perhaps I might get my "pot of gold" in the form of a good painting.

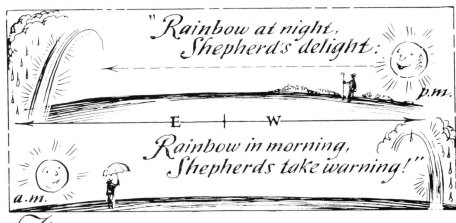

"Rainbow at night,
Shepherd's delight:

p.m.

E — W

a.m.

Rainbow in morning,
Shepherds take warning!"

This is true because nearly all showers move West to East

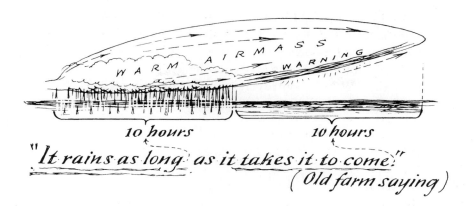

"It rains as long as it takes it to come."

(Old farm saying)

THE THIRD WEEK of July started with Saint Swithin's Day. If it rains on the fifteenth of July, according to an ancient saying, it will rain for forty days. Although everyone seems to know about Saint Swithin's Day, few people know how the legend began; fewer know anything about the good saint. He lived in the ninth century and died as the Bishop of Winchester. He was not canonized by the Church but he became a saint by popular acclaim. He was buried, according to his own will, outside the walls of the church, "where the rain could fall and comfort him." But on July 15, in the year 971, his body was removed and placed within the church, contrary to his express wishes. Thereby started the weather legend, for the instant his body was removed a terrible storm broke, which continued for forty days. The event became known as Bishop Swithin's Day and the rain legend continued to function until 1093, when the bishop was canonized by popular acclaim. And so the saying went:

> Saint Swithin's Day if thou dost rain,
> For forty days it will remain:
> Saint Swithin's Day if thou be fair,
> For forty days 'twill rain na mair.

The sixteenth of July gave us an eclipse of the moon and clear skies to observe it. It rose like a half moon and went back to a full moon by ten o'clock.

Even though it has been explained that there is nothing to it, there is still controversy about the moon's effect on weather. The men of science laugh it down as follows:

> *The moon and the weather*
> *May change together;*
> *But change of the moon*
> *Does not change the weather.*
> *If we'd no moon at all,*
> *And that may seem strange,*
> *We'd still enjoy weather*
> *That's subject to change.*

That poem, which meteorologists often refer to, is quite true; yet there are still some things I wonder about. If the moon causes tides in the fluid ocean of water that surrounds the earth, why does it not also cause greater tides in the even more fluid ocean of air that surrounds the earth? (Fluid, of course, means flowing—not liquid.) No new idea this, for Loomis's *Meteorology* of a hundred years ago tells of a "feeble lunar tide in the atmosphere, similar to that of the ocean." Today's research claims the tide is so feeble that no effect is exerted on actual weather. Yet I do believe that rain is most frequent at the turn of the tide (if the air is humid) and that this is the result of a sudden lowering of pressure caused by the displacement of tidal water by atmosphere.

Two more nights of clear air since Saint Swithin's Day. Perhaps for forty days " 'twill rain na mair." It is interesting to realize that the moon's face is so clear because there is not the blurring effect that would be there if the moon had atmosphere. The earth, if viewed from the moon, would be all one disc of brightness, with all the continents and geographical contours blotted out by a bright layer of air.

Moon weatherlore, I find, is scarce. The only sayings the almanacs have offered are, "Clear moon, frost soon," and "Sharp horns do threaten windy weather." "Sharp horns" are the points at both ends of a new to half moon: if they are clearly defined or "sharp," wind may be expected. "Fuzzy points" are caused by poor visibility through temperature inequalities at high altitude. Stars become very clear and the moon's horns distinct when high-altitude disturbances are washed away by strong winds. And those winds will normally descend to reach you by tomorrow.

I am going to take advantage of the clearness of the moon and the possibility of dry winds tomorrow. I shall varnish the guesthouse floor. The success of a painting job depends so much on weather, yet so few consider it. Painting on a humid day seals in the moisture; the paint dries on top but it stays wet underneath, never really drying.

How interesting it would be if weathermen gave their forecasts with suggestions for making use of the weather. Perhaps "Dry air tomorrow—a good day for painting and varnishing," or "Humid air expected tomorrow—a bad day for painting and varnishing." That sort of thing would mean more to the average person than the giving of mathematical barometric pressures and references to fronts and air masses that few readers understand.

The old almanacs described weather nicely and made you almost feel the air and see the sky; today's meteorologists tend to analyze the weather scientifically, and their reports are often dull. I should like to lend my library of old almanacs to any weathercaster so he may use some of the fine old phrases. Let's look at some rich wording from the *Clergyman's Almanac,* 1801:

Signs of an uncomfortable and driving rain.
Good haying weather.
Boisterous winds mixed with cheery flurries of snow.
The warm influences of the heavens give life and beauty to the day.
Thick air with appearances of thunder.

It is so easy to find fault with the poor weatherman! I wonder how often he finds fault with us. A city-bred meteorologist was once sent to the corn belt and found that the farmers there took their weather seriously, phoning in for information at all hours of the day and night. Hogs, he later learned, are butchered only when the weather is slated to be very cold. When a farmer phoned asking, "Is tomorrow going to be cold enough to kill my hogs?" the new weatherman could think of no reply but "Gosh—are hogs that delicate?"

*Sharp horns upon the moon—
Promise windy weather soon*

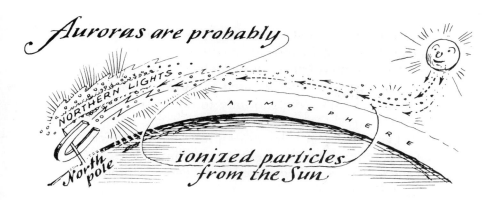

Auroras are probably ionized particles from the Sun

NORTHERN LIGHTS

North pole

ATMOSPHERE

A WEEK of dry weather. A very strong mass of cold air moved in from the northwest six days ago, persisting ever since, bringing six stinging blue skies with high cumulus puffs by day and six crystal jet skies at night. The first night's new air flow brought with it a faint auroral glow over the northern horizon. Although I have never heard it discussed before, I am sure that strong air flows from the north carry with them some of the electrified auroral particles that are abundant near the poles. The Northern Lights are not born in the north at all; they come from the sun and they first strike the earth near the equator. Because they are magnetized particles, they flow to the earth's magnets, the North and South Poles, collecting there as the Aurora Borealis at the North Pole and the Aurora Australis at the South Pole.

The auroral glow that came with this northern air mass was faint and noticeable only because I was looking for it. The nights that followed have been almost as cool as the days have been hot.

Nothing seems so sudden as a July shower. A few moments after it has gone, the skies give no trace of its having happened. It is odd that such downpours do so little toward filling reservoirs, or even raising the level of the smallest lakes. There is some small panic across the countryside about the shortage of water: the newspapers have urged people to take tub baths instead of showers. This is so wrong, because the impression of great waste during a shower bath is caused only by the great fall and noise of water. One time I measured the amount of water used in a prolonged shower; it would have filled the tub only to about two and a half inches!

These clear nights have been marked by a thick balm of dew that makes one feel that rain has fallen. And true to the folklore weather sign of heavy dew, the morning sun rises to another dry day. The most rain we can hope for, it seems, are July summer showers. They do not penetrate the ground deep enough to satisfy the farmers.

The dog days are with us. No two almanacs agree as to the exact date, but most of them put the beginning of dog days on July 26. Everyone talks about "dog days" but few know what the expression means. Some will tell you that it signifies hot sultry days "not fit for a dog"; others say it is the weather in which dogs go mad. Neither is correct, for the dog days are a period of from four to six weeks of warm weather that is marked by the rising of Sirius, the Dog Star. When this star rises in conjunction with the sun, the effects, according to the ancients, were droughts, plagues and madness; but as this occurs at different times in different latitudes and is constantly changing in any one region, the conflicting almanac dates are understandable.

hi! Dog Star!

Sirius, brightest star, and the Sun rise together during the Dog days.

".. dead bodies of Great Trees, still clad in their Armor of Bark."

MY ARTIST FRIEND Denver Gillen came by yesterday with his sketch pad to do some pictures of the old dead elm in the pasture. The tree is so near the spot where the rainbow of last month appeared that I decided to join him, to carry through with superstition and do a painting from that "end of the rainbow" site.

I have always neglected painting from nature and depended too much on my memory for outdoor scenes, so this painting period was more discipline than anticipated pleasure; yet I have never spent a better hour at work. It might well have been the "pot of gold" I expected to find, for making a painting of the old tree instilled in me a new interest and a more profound respect for trees.

It is strange how some dead trees are eyesores while others are outstandingly beautiful, their naked hulks silvering in the sun and the ground around them strewn with fallen boughs. I have often come upon a fallen giant of a tree in

125

the forest and the effect is like seeing the body of a dead prehistoric monster. Although I do not know why, it always commands a stop for inspection, a climb upon it and a walk along its wide trunk. The decay of these dead trees is surprisingly slow. Prostrate pines have been known to preserve their sap and lie amid rotting undergrowth for sixty years. And upright gray shafts, like the tree in my pasture, remain standing for a man's lifetime, until one comes to know them as familiarly as the living trees. You may pick out the branchless shafts of such hoary trees in the landscape of a mountain forest, and they stand out like guardians over the rest. A great tree never dies.

Now in August as some of the leaves are dying, the dead tree-giants look all the more at home in the tapestry of countryside. There are already patches of browning leaves to be seen on the wall of the opposite hillside. As a general rule, those trees which keep their leaves longest in autumn are the first to bud in spring.

July and August are very similar months, specializing in sultry weather. No matter how fine the day, you may usually see a brooding sky over an August horizon.

The thing that I remember most about August, however, is its flowers. The purple asters and the many kinds of orange and red flowers that all seem to smell alike recall my past more than anything else. These end-of-summer flowers, the sound of distant thunder, the smell of dry earth and the drowsiness of late vacation days are things which will come back to you years later with startling clarity, although at the time they seem insignificant.

When I was five years old a farmer's wife taught me a rhyme about thunder. It went:

The lightning is the yaller gal that lives up in the cloud,
The thunder is the black man that hollers out loud.
The thunder kisses the yaller gal and thinks he is a wonder,
He bumps his head against a cloud and that's what makes
    the thunder.

All these years have I remembered this ditty, though I have never heard it elsewhere. I have often wondered where it originated, whether it was Negro or from New England. But in one of my old almanacs I now find the following weather-folklore poem:

Yaller gal, yaller gal, flashin' through the night,
Summer storms will pass you by unless the lightning's white.

Nowhere else have I seen reference to lightning as a yellow girl, but the idea is entrancing. White lightning, I recall, is usually lightning of a storm on its way, while red or yellow lightning is so often "heat lightning" or the distant reflection of summer storms in the east or south that are already passing you by.

You might wonder why heat lightning appears only at night. The reason is simply that only the darkness of night makes the long-distance reflection of light possible.

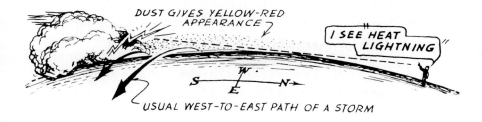

DUST GIVES YELLOW-RED APPEARANCE

I SEE HEAT LIGHTNING

USUAL WEST-TO-EAST PATH OF A STORM

Second Week of August

THE LAST RAINFALL was ten days ago and that, the newspapers tell me, was an immeasurable amount. This week last August, it stated, Connecticut had 3.1 inches of rain. I have no mental picture of "3.1 inches of rain" and I do wish the weather bureau would devise another way to measure rainfall. I recall a shower, in which only 2.4 inches had fallen, that sank my rowboat.

There are so many popular measurements which are incomprehensible to the human mind and therefore have no impact on our imaginations. The word "billion" is a good example of what I mean, for no one can imagine what a billion of anything would look like. To my knowledge, no wheel has ever turned a billion times. If it were possible for a fast plane to fly full speed for a year, its propeller would not have turned a billion times! A billion new one-dollar bills in a stack would make a pile six and a half miles high. To make this word more distressing, a billion in America is a thousand millions but a billion in England is a million millions!

The *Old Farmer's Almanac* says of August, "Now go roll in the clover, the summer's near over." I don't know whether it means for the reader to roll in the clover or if it implies that the clover should be gathered. I chose the first meaning and so walked to the hilltop this morning, where I relaxed in a choice clover bed while Nimbo investigated an old woodchuck burrow. The ground is dry by feel and smell, and there seems no promise of rain.

The papers are full of rain-making stories. Although there is small proof of its exact importance, the rain-making business continues. Based on the fact that cloud seeding can modify certain storms that already exist, research in cloud seeding continues. Washington's official report (United States Department of Commerce, August 1948) was that ". . . there is little evidence to suggest cloud-seeding initiates self-propagating storms. The methods are certainly not promising for the relief of drought."

Typical of the thousands of lawsuits against "rain-makers" is the case of Kiutus Tecumseh, an Indian who sued the Big Bend Water Development Company in Yakima Valley, Washington. Their man-made rain, Tecumseh charged, caused him to lose his crop of hay. Reading this took me back many years to Taos, before that New Mexico town became an artist's bohemia. Since I was a young art student, my Indian neighbor Tony Luhan (husband of Mabel) asked me to paint a decoration on his new automobile. I painted a thunderbird with outstretched wings, and Tony went off proudly. At that time the thunderbird was the only Indian symbol I knew, but I wasn't aware that it symbolized rain. Tony's destination was Phillips's ranch, where a rodeo was being held and where he wanted to show off his shiny new LaSalle. I shall never forget his returning, both he and the LaSalle covered with mud from a sudden mountain rainstorm. "Take thunderbird off my car," said Tony. "Look what thunderbird rain sign did for me!"

Thunderbird

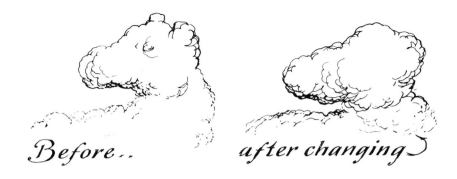

Before..   *after changing*

**Third
Week
of
August**

I RECALL that on summer evenings of my youth, when I sat on the porch with my family, we made a game of picking out odd shapes in the night shadows. There were always animal figures or strange heads to be found in the outlines of the trees. I still see shapes in clouds while observing the clouds, and often find them popping up in my paintings. In painting cloudscapes, one of the things I now avoid is letting a cloud assume a suggestive shape. I once did a cloud mural that featured a lofty thunderhead. The buyer was very pleased with it. But when I looked at it later, I pointed out to him the fact that the thunderhead was shaped like the head of a hippopotamus. A year later, the owner of the mural wrote to me, asking me to change the cloud. "Since you called it to my attention," he said "every time I look at the confounded painting, I see a hippopotamus instead of a cloud!"

Tomorrow I go fishing. For the first time in about twenty years I shall use worms. The story around here is that the biggest trout and bass are biting on worms and in very deep water. The reason is interesting. It seems that there are less and less insects each year, and whereas the big fish used to feed on flies, they have become tired of waiting for flies that never show up and have gone to deep-water feeding grounds, and they have changed their menu.

One of the insects that I thought was disappearing is the

130

tick; this year my dog has been entirely free of them. But the real reason is that my dog has moved from Long Island. There, the ticks have been multiplying yearly for the past hundred years. Lion Gardiner brought ticks to America in 1642 when he imported cattle from England for his herds on Gardiners Island. The cattle roamed the woods and infested the wild deer with ticks, and the deer swam to the mainland. That, according to an old tale, is how Long Island became infested with those ugly insects.

I wonder if there is a connection between the scarcity of insects nowadays and the change in the seasons. I recall as a child how nights in the country were made lively by the buzzing of what we called "June bugs," and the thudding of big beetles that seemed destined to complete each flight with some sort of head-on collision. Because of these memories of early summer, I moved to the country prepared to meet all kinds of insects during June. It is now the middle of August and not even one beetle has shown up.

As I write this, my window opens into the night air and a forest of summer noises. My light is bright and there is no screen, yet only three very small moths keep me company. I am sure that thirty years ago there must have been more bugs in the world. Or are things just amplified by the looming world of past memories? It seems to me that snow was deeper, wind stronger, and thunder louder once upon a time. But a few years ago I revisited the place of my childhood summers and saw what had once been my bedroom. The shock has stayed with me, for what I once thought to be a very large room was a very tiny one. From that moment I realized that everything must seem so much larger to children, and that things also loom larger in our screen of memory as the years pass by.

Actually things do not change as much as we sometimes think. It is good and satisfying in these days of wondering if atomic blasts are affecting the weather, or if the seasons are changing, to glance through the old almanacs and find that the weather two hundred years ago was not too different from our present-day weather. I pick at random for the third week of July, 1756, "scattered showers along the seacoast but some drought in New England," which coincides with today's report. Or I look at my weather map for today and find thunderstorm symbols scattered along the coast; they are the exact same symbols that the ancient Pueblo Indians used. I'm not sure why, but that's comforting.

BY FACING THE WIND AND POINTING TO MY RIGHT, I LOCATE THE STORM "EYE"

WIND

MONTAUK

The counterclockwise winds of a storm

THE END of August. Today's New York newspapers say that this morning in Connecticut will be fair, cloudy and cool. It is ten o'clock at the moment, and the rain, which started slowly last night, has now reached the torrent stage. The wind is beyond gale force, reaching gusts of fifty miles an hour. Evidently the tropical cyclone heading this way has moved inland and northward faster than the weather bureau predicted.

By facing the wind and pointing outward with your right hand you can always find the nearest low-pressure or storm-center area. During a hurricane, this rule is invaluable, for you can really pinpoint the hurricane's center or "eye." By knowing the natural hurricane path (usually northward and then eastward), you can then ascertain if the storm center has reached you or has passed on.

At noon I went outside and faced the wind, finding the storm center on my right, which was toward the east or directly off Montauk Point. The hurricane must have traveled much faster than the textbooks say hurricanes should go, possibly approaching sixty miles an hour. My barograph has shown a steady but erratic decline, a definite hurricane pattern. But a sharp incline has marked the

**Last
Week
of
August**

133

passing of the "eye"; the storm has passed its peak. Barometers can often be misleading and unreliable, but when the weather is severe they are more exact and informative.

Hurricanes can be likened to phonograph records, which turn at the same speed but may be moved from room to room or left standing still. Usually hurricanes pinwheel their winds steadily over a hundred miles an hour, while the entire "pinwheel" mechanism moves at only five to fifteen miles an hour. Over the flat sea they move fastest; over rough terrain they tend to deteriorate. This storm must have traveled well out to sea on its journey up here, picking up speed over the open water. Pity the poor weatherman, who gets the blame after a weather disaster!

Within the next year or so we might see our coastlines scattered with radar stations for the purpose of spotting storm centers, to gauge their speed more accurately. But even radar cannot predict in advance whether hurricanes will stand still, move slowly or zip by. Improved weather predictions, in my estimation, are limited to better and faster communications. There will always be some uncertainties connected with the weather.

The north-light window I put in my barn studio is straining under the wind; the rain has already leaked through it in a few places. I have often wondered why the artist has so many things against him; right in the wall that should be most insulated against cold and storm, he places a large north window.

The hills of Connecticut cause enough friction to lessen the speed of hurricane winds; at least there seemed to be less trees down during this blow. Oddly enough, the greatest damage to my trees turned out to be no damage at all; rather was it a help. Two large dead limbs on my butternut tree had been too high and difficult to reach with a pruning saw; now they are down. Several limbs that were growing too close to the house were also taken care of. It made me think that hurricanes were possibly meant to do good rather than to destroy. The Maker simply didn't take man and his church steeples and yachts and houses into consideration. I think He might have had the forests in mind when He devised storms. Even the direction of hurricane wind seems designed for proper pruning, for it pinwheels so that whatever is in its path is hit first from one side and then the other. Anyone who uses a rotary lawn mower knows what a thorough job such an action does.

Despite the tragedy of hurricane stories, there is always a bit of humor too. On a small farm north of here, a bridge was blown away, but the same storm toppled a silo across the brook and made a fine covered bridge almost in the same place.

The only damage to a big neon sign on Route 7 which spelled out MILK SHAKES was that the middle bar in the letter H shifted, making it into an N. So we are all amused at the new sign which advertises MILK SNAKES.

after the storm..... The Silo Bridge

Alto-cumulus-Castellatus   Lenticular   Mammatus

**First
Week
of
September**

A NEW TENANT has come to Weather Hill. A friend has left a cat to keep my dog Nimbo company. We have named it Cirro to match Nimbo in meteorological flavor. The "nimbus" cloud, incidentally, is no more—it has been struck from weather nomenclature. Up until a few years ago, the word "nimbus" was the most used cloud name. Now it is only a defining prefix or suffix as in "cumulonimbus" (rainy cumulus) and "nimbo-stratus" (rainy stratus).

Most weather books explain that the word "nimbus" was derived from a word meaning "rain," but its original meaning was "halo" or "luminous headdress." Therefore any cloud which has assumed a lofty head (which results in rain) becomes a nimbus type.

Some of the Latin cloud names for cumulus types are more picturesque than identifying. The alto-cumulus-castellatus clouds are castlelike or turreted; cumulus-lenticularis clouds are lentil-shaped, lenslike or flattish and ovate; cumulo-mammatus hang downward like mammary glands or breasts.

An interesting incident of the week was finding the kitchen attic filled with nuts, obviously put there by squirrels. One side of the floor, however, was filled with hickory nuts, while the other side had only walnuts. I asked Jimmy if squirrels sorted out nuts in that manner and he told me he had often seen that very same thing. His explanation, however, was that trees have cycles in bearing and that perhaps one pile represented a good season of walnut gathering, while the other pile represented a later good year for hickory nuts.

136

I learned about cycles in tree crops when I first came to Weather Hill. The big walnut tree had covered the lawn beneath it with five bushels of nuts. This winter the same tree had exactly nine nuts. So Jimmy's explanation is most plausible.

One of the chores of moving into an old house is ridding it of squirrels and mice. Frankly I like them and I enjoy watching them at their antics. They are at the same time friend and enemy to man's interests. They eat insects both good and bad, and they eat the seed of both pest-weed and grain. I cannot help but feel sorry for the tiny fellows whenever I hear a mousetrap spring in some remote part of the house. True to an old Christmas tradition, I closed all the traps at Weather Hill on Christmas and left a good-sized piece of cheese there with the compliments of Saint Nicholas.

The common house mouse is an emigrant from Europe and was introduced to New England during the Revolution. The mice that have found their way to my house have all been woodland mice, which seems to give them a special dignity. Here I have caught deer mice, woodland jumping mice, pine mice, meadow mice and lemming mice, but I like the deer mouse best of all; it is the clown of the mouse world. Its body is three inches long while its tail is over eight; it can leap more than ten feet. My dog Nimbo enjoys them as much as I do. Although I am certain he could catch them with very little effort, he has extraordinary and animated chases after them which always end up with the mouse disappearing in the high grass.

Young deer mice are so light in weight that they can go from grass stalk to grass stalk like an insect without bending or breaking it. I have seen them go along a slender stem, picking up the dew on it, in the early morning. These dry days offer so little water that dew is probably the only drink of the living things in the fields. By now, the nights are almost as long as the days, and "dews of September" are almost as wetting as the night rains of June.

When I studied meteorology, it was always difficult for me to realize that clouds cannot form in clear air and that precipitation must have something to form upon before it can be born. As an example my teacher used dew, which is liquid moisture born of air only when it has something to be born upon. A glass of iced liquid, with dew forming on its cold sides, demonstrates perfectly this rule of meteorology.

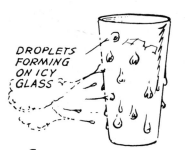

DROPLETS FORMING ON ICY GLASS

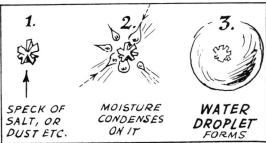

1. SPECK OF SALT, OR DUST ETC.

2. MOISTURE CONDENSES ON IT

3. WATER DROPLET FORMS

Cloud droplets and precipitation do not occur in clear air — they must form upon something

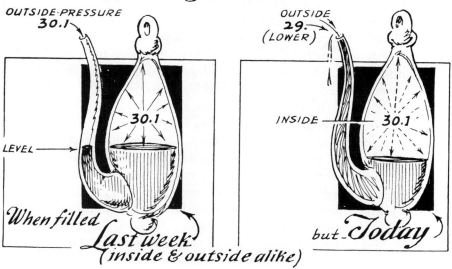

How the "Cape Cod Glass" works...

OUTSIDE·PRESSURE
30.1

OUTSIDE
29. (LOWER)

30.1

INSIDE —— 30.1

LEVEL ——→

When filled Last week
(inside & outside alike)

but Today

Overcast and still. The weather reports have alerted the countryside for rain and hurricane winds. My barometer is acting nervous and the inked line is jerking steadily downhill. The Cape Cod barometer, which is no precision instrument, has not yet reacted, but it will be interesting to see what it will do in real low pressure.

My Cape Cod glass is filled with some red-colored water and the air pressure of the day I set it, both trapped inside. When the outside pressure changes against the inside pressure, the water in the spout responds by rising and lowering. In very low pressure, it is supposed not only to rise but overflow.

New England has previously had hurricane protection both from its sheltering hills and from the polar air stream, which tended to guide hurricanes northward in an oceanward arc. But since 1938 the polar air stream has shifted, and all of our East Coast has become a vulnerable playground for tropical cyclones.

The early winds this year have put many of the apple crops on the ground before they were ripe. Yet it is said that wind and strain on a tree will improve its fruit. In looking up accounts of bygone hurricanes, I found reports of second crops of fruit caused by the effects of a strong wind. After the destructive hurricane in Louisiana during the first three days of September in 1772, mulberry trees blossomed and bore a second crop. Cited by Blodgett from the historical writings of Ramsay and Gayarre, a hurricane at Charleston on September 15, 1752, stripped all the leaves from orchards; yet the trees blossomed again and bore unusually large and delicious fruit in the very late autumn.

The lull before a storm is always dramatic in its hush. Outdoors this morning, you got the impression that nature was holding its breath before it took a wild plunge across the countryside. Indian lore credits this calm as a time for silent prayer that the Sky God allows before he makes his attack. Actually, it is only a period of wind-shift before an approaching front or a new weather pattern.

The stillness today is not heralding a new front; it is preceding a massive low-pressure system. Although the trees are hardly stirring, there is a steady movement of high stratus clouds from the east. Reports have plotted the storm center just south of New England. The weather vanes on the barns in the valley seem poised for a change: the motionless chanticleer on farmer Wanzer's roof looks as though it is listening for the wind to come. A train rattles across the silent landscape, sounding as if it were only a mile away instead of five; its whistle and a puff of steam lag behind long after it has disappeared.

A great flock of birds roosted this morning on the trees along the ridge of the lake, true to an old folklore hurricane tradition. I do not know if there is any scientific truth in it, but inasmuch as lowering pressure might make it more difficult for flight, or at least make it necessary for a bird to beat his wings faster through the thinning air, perhaps birds do choose to rest more at this time. An old sailing rhyme mentions it:

> *The glass is down, the gulls are flocked along the shore,*
> *The clouds are low'ring fast and soon the wind will roar.*

Dr. Jenner speaks of the uncertain flight of birds during pressure changes in his "Signs of Rain":

> *. . . and see yon rooks, how odd their flight!*
> *They imitate the gliding kite,*
> *And seem precipitate to fall,*
> *As if they felt the piercing ball.*
> *'Twill surely rain, I see with sorrow,*
> *Our jaunt must be put off tomorrow.*

Before the blow

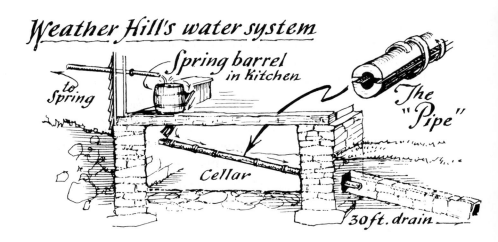

Weather Hill's water system

Spring barrel in kitchen

to Spring

The "Pipe"

Cellar

30 ft. drain

Third Week of September

A WET WEEK for Weather Hill. The torrents of rain filled the cellar, which has the original dirt floor. But I remembered having Earl plug up an unexplainable square hole in the lower part of one foundation wall, and suddenly came to the conclusion that I had closed some sort of drain-off for water. By opening it again, I not only dried the cellar but reconstructed the planning of the ancient water system of the house. There had been a hollowed-log water-pipe system from the kitchen spring barrel, leading into the cellar and out the square lead-off tunnel. The whole system was below the level of the ground and protected from freezing, and spring water flowed into the kitchen all year around. One of my almanacs explains the merit of underground water pipes nicely, saying, "The seasons are reversed twenty feet down, the soil temperature there being coldest in June and warmest in January."

The section of wooden water pipe I found was unlike anything I have heard of. It was a round pole that had been sawed in half and then grooved "hollow" before being put back together again. It had then been wrapped with splint or willow bark. I suppose the very fact of the wood's being wet insured against leakage. This early pipe not only made use of the only thing available; wood was also the best material, outlasting iron.

After a storm, people are so much more sociable, comparing accounts of the damage and swapping anecdotes. Weather Hill has had a steady flow of tradesmen and neighbors who borrow shovels, offer to help, and despite the tracking of mud about the place, keep me in good spirits.

Had coffee with the garbage man today. His name is Percy. Garbage men in the city look like garbage men, but country garbage collection is done by "truckers," who amaze me with their gentility and neat manner of working. They put refuse in paper bags and stack them up to look like a truckload of valuable merchandise. Percy is a fine farm boy who is saving his salary to buy a piece of land in the valley. He knocked at the door to inform me that he had been "unthoughtful about leaving a bill, so here was one I fetched up." So I asked him in for coffee and enjoyed a pleasant ten minutes, also a full half hour later in trying to recall the rich phrases and Yankeeisms he had spoken. These of course, I added to my collection of New England language.

The Yankee countryman is a great inventor of words. When he comes to a verbal impasse, he will likely come up with a word of his own. Most Southern backwoods slang is of Elizabethan origin, but New England country language is always self-styled.

I am sure that much of our slang of a hundred years to come will be derived from that all-American source, the soda fountain. One of the pleasant things about New Milford is the soda fountain manned by women who do not "draw a brew," "shoot a coke" or "pour a Grade A." I've copied down some "drugstore language" and it is interesting to note that it is understood in just about any city in the United States. Try these out on your soda fountain:

"Shoot one" (a small coke).
"Grade A" (a glass of milk).
"Draw one" (a cup of coffee).
"LT down" (lettuce and tomato, toasted).
"Burn one" (malted drink).
"Freeze one" (frosted drink).
"Burn a Britisher" (English muffin).
"Eighty-one" (glass of water).

The weather is clearing. The winds are changing from southerly to westerly, which is a clockwise change known as "veering." (A counterclockwise change is called "backing.") This does not sound confusing, but it can be. Many a new air pilot will look at a wind-tee on the ground and forget momentarily whether it points at the direction of the wind, or flies with it. Many a person thinks that the arrow of a weather vane shows the direction in which the wind is flowing instead of pointing toward where it comes from.

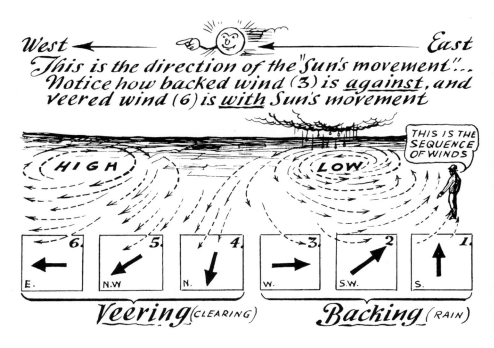

West ← *This is the direction of the "Sun's movement"...* → East
Notice how backed wind (3) is against, and veered wind (6) is with Sun's movement

HIGH　　　LOW

THIS IS THE SEQUENCE OF WINDS

| 6. | 5. | 4. | 3. | 2. | 1. |
| E. | N.W | N. | W. | S.W. | S. |

Veering (CLEARING)　　*Backing* (RAIN)

If you point at where the wind was, and then at where it comes from now, and your arm has moved clockwise, the wind has veered. "A veering wind will clear the sky," an old saying goes, "and a backing wind says storms are nigh."

An easier way to determine a veering or backing wind is to use the saying, "Winds that change against the sun, and winds that bring the rain are one." That is, a wind that blows against the sun's apparent movement from east to west is backing (stormy). When the wind begins to flow with the sun's movement again, it is veering to a change for the better.

The old Stove Chimney — new roof — Attic — Oak Platform

Last Week of September

Autumn begins on September the twenty-second. The maples have already been touched by gold, and the sounds of the forest and roadside are becoming dry and crackling. John Burroughs calls September the month of tall weeds. All along the stone walls here the ragweed, pigweed, burdock, asters, thistles and goldenrod have grown to giant proportions to join the spectacle of autumn. They no longer sway as they did in spring but bend stiffly now whenever a breeze stirs.

It is remarkable that many so-called American weeds came from the Old World, following the white man across the Atlantic. The dandelion, nettle, thistle, corn cockle, acrid buttercup, pigweed, plaintain, mallow, mayweed, the wild versions of parsnips, garlic, flax, mustard and radish, and countless others were unknown to the American Indian, all being introduced by the settlers.

The shepherd's-purse is common to China and the Jimson weed to Abyssinia. Some American plants have likewise been carried, probably in shipments of tobacco and maize, to Europe, where they have now become naturalized. It was once a custom never to throw a seed away but always to properly bury it. A hundred years ago when you ate plums or peaches, you always dug a small hole with your heel by the roadside and deposited the pit; many tree-lined

146

roads of yesterday were the result of this habit.

Emerson said a weed is a plant whose virtues have not yet been discovered, but John Burroughs referred to weeds as the tramps of the vegetable world. They steal rides, travel by boat and rail; they attach their seeds to your clothing or your dog's fur, and they travel even by flood and wind. But like true tramps they find travel easiest on the highway, and you will find them clustered there along every road, waiting for a ride.

The weeds are alive now with insects. Crickets, katydids and grasshoppers keep the thickets alive both night and day. The katydids rasp away as long as there is warmth to keep them going. As September closes and the nights become cooler, these insect thermometers keep accurate cadence with the seasons. "Katy-did-it" dwindles to "Katy-did," then to "Katy" and finally in October, a cold and hoarse "Kate," called out infrequently like a word spoken by someone asleep. We are told, as though it is not remarkable, how insects make noise by rubbing parts of their bodies together. Inasmuch as man cannot duplicate this acoustical action, and because I cannot conceive of only two tiny legs rubbing together to produce a sound that carries so far, I think it most remarkable. I recall being lost in a foggy night on the water; my only means of determining the direction of land was listening to the katydids and crickets almost a mile away.

Earl began a distasteful job at Weather Hill which I had been putting off until the very last. It is the removal of an obsolete chimney in the attic. This chimney starts in the attic, where ducts met from the flues of four Franklin stoves. This arrangement was the last word in farmhouse architecture in 1782, when this house was built. Somewhere along the line of years, when the iron heating stoves were removed, a new roof was built, covering the obsolete chimney and making it no more than a pile of useless bricks weighing down on the floor in the attic. I looked forward to finding treasure in the old chimney, but all that Earl unearthed was a swarm of ladybugs.

Ladybugs, which once were so rare that children made a wish when they found one, began swarming this year in March and have kept the roses of Weather Hill free of aphids all summer. The farm magazines mention sales of ladybugs by the gallon (about a quarter of a million bugs make up a gallon). They are harvested by special vacuum cleaner at migration spots in the Southwest, and sold to farmers to exterminate aphids and other pest bugs.

The word "ladybug" is a derivation of the true name, "ladybird," which was originally called "bird of Our Lady," referring to the Virgin Mary. The superstitions about these attractive little bugs are many. If you find one in your house on a winter's day, it is said, you will receive as many dollars as there are spots on its back. The habit of holding one on your finger tips and telling it to "fly away home" comes from an early Valentine superstition that the ladybug will fly in the direction of your lover.

This rich month of crickets and goldenrod, of drowsy days beneath a toasting sun, is fast closing the curtain on summer. The *New England Almanac* for 1851 says, "Ideal time for clearing the land, scything dry weeds from near farm buildings and protecting against autumn fires." Jimmy and a farm hand are tearing down some old henhouses behind Weather Hill that are a fire hazard. I put in a day helping them and enjoyed working in the high grass under the dry September sun, and felt years younger for it.

The henhouses were not ancient but they have been unused for many years, and the trees and weeds have taken over the entire scene. With the weeds gone it is interesting to note how much like the modern ranch house is the plain old-time chicken house. Put a picture window in the big wired opening, and a television antenna on top, and you have a typical modern small-home design. My henhouses even had solar roofs.

Modern solar buildings are not as new as one might think. A farm manual of 1815 speaks of such a henhouse with "an overhanging roof that slants upward, which lets the low winter sun in, and keeps the high summer sun out."

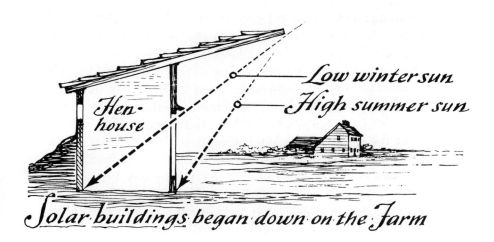

Solar buildings began down on the Farm

Locomobile 1920 b.c.
(before Chromium)

Gʀᴀʏ ʜᴀɪʀ or stiffness in the joints may be over-looked but it often takes the littlest thing to make you realize your age. This week I felt very old because I went out looking for a professional carriage-striper and couldn't find one. I don't like chromium and thought I might have it removed from my station wagon and painted stripes put there instead. The first car I drove was a Locomobile and I recall the striping on it as if it were yesterday. When chromium came in, the striper, I guess, went out. Everyone I discussed this matter with acted as though I were talking about something of a hundred years ago. I found no striper, so I shall do the job myself.

It occurs to me that the average automobile owner pays from ten to a hundred dollars for chromium advertisements and manufacturer's nameplates on his car, for which he should be paid instead of having to pay. Furthermore he is not asked if he likes chromium, yet he must pay hundreds of dollars for ornamental chromium whether he wants it or not. It seems extraordinary, also, that a sane adult will accept imitation engine exhaust holes in front fenders, imitation jet intakes and fins in rear fenders, even fake rocket nozzles, and not mind paying for it. Any day I expect the American automotive industry to introduce chromium fox tails as standard design. It seems such a pity to spoil beautifully streamlined simplicity with "ice-wagon" type of decoration.

With September over, summer's gardens have now spent themselves. There is a pleasing sadness about the drone of bees wandering among dried stalks and withered leaves. Yet there still are a few summer flowers blooming out of season, and the flowers of autumn with pungent, clean, cinnamon smells. Apples fall with sharp thuds to startle the quiet of summer's wake and to start the long procession of autumn sounds. Most people think of Indian summer for its bright colors, but it is something that the countryman can also feel and hear. All along the peaceful back roads where recently the noises of everyday life were muffled out by the canopy of green leaves, new sounds are beginning to creep through the bare branches. It sounds strange to hear the clucking of chickens, the droning of faraway automobile motors and the small noises of distant farm life as they invade the quiet glens of summer. Not loud noises, all hushed, but noticeable because they are different from summer sounds. A few days ago I walked along the edge of the lake and was treated to the crunch and rustle of leaves with each step I made. The acoustics of this season are different and all sounds, no matter how hushed, are as crisp as autumn air.

"Feeling" Indian summer is harder to explain than "hearing" it. About a half mile from my house there is a small group of summer cottages, which I came upon suddenly while walking. The ominous quiet of closed and shut-up houses can be as startling as a live thing. I am sure that a house in hibernation does not affect everyone in such a manner, but some houses are so full of having been lived in, that they speak to me as plainly as humans. In Indian summer, there is a quiet aliveness over the whole countryside. There is an unhappy shutting of houses and a forgetting of summer, and although nature does its best to coax the summer people back, it must be content to settle down for the winter with its own, the people who live with it year round. How glad I am that I am one of these. Yet I am left with a melancholy for all those who cannot enjoy the season with me.

A neighboring farmer put it nicely when he said, "City folks like green around them. When the leaves begin to turn they think it's a sign to go home. A week or two after they've left, the hills break out in colors they never saw before. With cornfields full of punkins by day and the haze of harvest moon by night—why, New England ain't even ripe until after they've gone home!" It seems that nature is putting its heart into a superb performance for an all too empty house.

The Virginia creeper has now turned scarlet; when its leaves fall, the farmers say that summer has truly ended. The yellowwood, tulip and ironwood have turned yellow. Soon they will stand out like golden patches in the carpeted hills of red. Actually there are no definite rules about trees changing their specific colors in autumn; each year they are liable to change to a slightly different shade, or to do so in different steps. When the summer has been particularly hot or winds have been strong enough to injure the trees, foliage turns earlier and it assumes a deeper shade. I recall the greatest show of color was after a severe hurri-

"Nothing gives more yet asks less in return."
Jonathan Chapman
"Johnny Appleseed"

cane season, when all the most brilliant leaves were growing from split or fallen trees.

The dictionary tells me that there is no record of the origin of the name Indian summer, but my almanacs speak frequently of "Red Man's Summer," and the "Indian Firefogs of late autumn." This substantiates tales I have heard of how the early settlers mistook the haze of late New England autumn air for the campfires of marauding Indians. I can readily understand how those people, who must have been always on the alert for Indian attacks, might have been startled by the strange smokelike haze of this season.

"Summer clouds hold their heads high"
INDIAN·SAYING

Winter   Summer

Second Week of October

THE UNTIMELY WARMTH of Indian summer brings out many of the creatures associated with spring. Today I saw clouds of gnats dancing among the bare alder branches. Field crickets, whose cadence was slowed by the first weeks of cool September air, quicken their song now for a last encore. Confused spring peepers can often be heard during broad daylight. Fish venture toward the shore and sun themselves in water so shallow that their fins protrude above the surface.

This is the brief time of year when the sky, too, masquerades as summertime. Warm-weather cumulus clouds are seen at midday, but the sky is swept clean and blue again by night. Cold weather is not far over the horizon. In another month the whole theater of cloudform will have lowered to its winter height, about a thousand feet lower for the low clouds and about a half mile lower for the high clouds.

Yesterday I walked to the lake to contemplate the chore of pulling up the boats, but decided to let them stay in the water until really cold weather. It is so good to be boating in the crisp cold air of late autumn, and you are usually alone then with your pleasure. When I returned home I got sweaters and warm clothing out of the camphored cases in the attic. I never cease to enjoy that aroma. The old-timers here used to pack woolens away with cedar chips and pine needles; there are still traces of it between some of the wide floor boards. Attics are such warehouses of memories; I seldom go into Weather Hill's attic without staying longer than I expected to. This time I became fascinated by the reading matter in the ancient Connecticut newspapers that are pasted wallpaper-fashion on parts of the ceiling. I found one advertisement from a Stonington firm offering an "absolute weather predictor" for one dollar. "A magic liquid," the ad stated, "that clouds up when it is about to rain." I wonder if this could be shark-liver oil. Captain Young, who wrote "Shark, Shark," once told me that natives of the South Seas used bottled shark-liver oil in this manner to predict weather, but I have never heard it mentioned elsewhere.

Just reading the advertisements in an early Connecticut newspaper is suitable entertainment for any winter's evening.

These hills of Connecticut specialized in manufacturing the things that the famed Yankee peddlers carried. The advertisements in the old newspapers must have been written by Yankee peddlers too. I am frank to admit that the salesmanship employed by some of the ads has often had me reaching for my pen and checkbook before I could remember that the newspaper is over a century old.

Tales of Connecticut salesmanship are entertaining and occasionally true. One apple orchard near Danbury is said to have been struck badly by hail: the usually smooth red surface of all the apples had become pitted and blemished by hailstones. Not to be ruined by a little thing like that, the farmer wrapped each apple in a fine tissue paper that bore the legend HAIL KISSED APPLES, *the fruit with a heavenly taste.* Then he doubled the price of his apples and is said to have done very well. Another farmer placed advertisements in all the leading farm journals, offering a prize of ten dollars for the best apple. "Send as many as you please," the ad read, "size, flavor or texture might be the winning factor. There are ribbons for second and third prizes." Outside of picking one farmer's name at random each year and sending him a ten-dollar bill, our Yankee schemer had little else to do than to unwrap thousands of the country's best apples. He was in the fruit business and selling prize fruit without even owning an orchard!

Virgil Geddes, who happens to be my Brookfield postmaster and author of *Country Postmaster*, has many interesting tales about Connecticut schemers. He tells me about one get-rich-quick planner who came to him with the idea of placing advertisements in all the cheap magazines, offering "dirty postcards for sale at one dollar each." In return, his plan was to send plain penny postcards, but all scuffed and smudged, very dirty indeed. Would this be breaking any law? Would it be misrepresenting? Virgil, who wanted no part of it, suggested that he write to Washington to find out.

Friends who have heard that I am compiling this almanac have been sending me whatever old almanacs they happen upon and my collection is growing fast. There are so many kinds of almanacs that I keep them arranged by type rather than by date. More recent ones advertise patent medicines, but in the beginning, all kinds of businesses and organizations put out their own almanacs. Picking a handful at random, I find *The Clergyman's Almanac, The Musician's Almanac, Clark's Anti-Bilious Almanac, The Farmer's Friend, Light of the World, The Merchant's Almanac, Miner's Almanac* and *Planter's Almanac*. There was almost no end.

The almanac was the magazine of yesteryear; it must have had great use during long winter nights on the farm. The title page of the current *Old Farmer's Almanac* (published by Yankee Inc., Dublin, New Hampshire) embraces the formula for all the earlier ones: ". . . containing, besides the large number of astronomical calculations and the farmer's calendar for every month in the year, a variety of new, useful and entertaining matter."

Sometimes hearing about people is of greater and more lasting interest than meeting them. A man living somewhere on the opposite hill has expressed his wish, through the grapevine of tradesmen, to visit Weather Hill. He has moved here from the city and he enjoys old houses. So far as I know, he has retired from work; his claim to fame hereabouts is nothing more than a ham which hangs in his cellar. They tell me that he always wanted to live where he could hang a ham in the cellar the way the old-timers used to. Now he has his ham and he gets the greatest satisfaction out of going downstairs whenever he wishes and cutting a big piece from it. I am sure he could never equal this rich picture of himself, and I think I prefer just thinking of him as the man with the ham.

I found an ancient ham hook in the attic and shall either send it to my interesting neighbor, or start the winter with a ham of my own.

Weather Hill's ham hook

Cyclonic wind -- Nature's mixing bowl

Third Week of October

THE WEATHER REPORTS tell of a concentrated low-pressure area taking the "hurricane track" up the east coast. I looked outside tonight and noticed a wan moon within a haloed sky, the same as last night. A halo merely indicates a spreading of cirroform ice clouds, but a persistence of this occurrence is unusual and means a particularly large pin-wheeling of high clouds.

Earl came by to do some chores, but with another big wind coming, he decided to get back home and ready things for it. I insisted he have coffee with me and we had a very informative chat: it is amusing how much we learn ourselves when trying to explain things to others. Earl asked me what a hurricane is and I chose a salad bowl to demonstrate cyclonic action. Not till then did I realize that cyclones are nature's mixing bowls of the atmosphere. Moisture from here, dust from there, seeds and pollen from faraway places, everything gets mixed around and inward toward the storm center, contributing to the processes of life.

I believe if children were given such similes they might conceive of the necessity of storms and lose fear of them. A neighbor is teaching her children to enjoy rainy days, saving special treats for bad weather. Whereas most children sulk and fret when it rains, her children actually look forward to it. Instead of:

Rain rain go away
Come again another day.

she has taught her children:

> *To talk of the weather is nothing but folly;*
> *When it rains on the hill, the sun's in the valley.*

One of the standard "things to say" about the weather is
the one about the rain at least being good for the farmers.
In 1763, Boswell remarked that "the rain is at least good
for the vegetable kingdom." Dr. Johnson replied, "Why yes,
sir, it is good for vegetables, and for the animals who eat
those vegetables, and for the animals who eat those animals."

Old dogs have so often been given credit for forecasting
storms. As Dr. Jenner said in observing prestorm signs:

> *My dog, so altered in his taste,*
> *Quits mutton bones on grass to feast.*

There are three explanations as to why an approaching
storm might be felt by a dog before it would affect a human.
First, a lowering of air pressure releases captive odors and
scents that only dogs are aware of. Secondly, the difference
in sound echoes in humid air and a lowering ceiling might
be first noticed by a dog's sensitive ears. Thirdly, and particularly with Dr. Jenner's dog who feasted on grass, low
pressure and moist air intensifies rheumatic pain. Dr. Jenner further observed:

> *Hark how the chairs and tables crack!*
> *Old Betty's joints are on the rack;*
> *Her corns with shooting pains torment her*
> *And to her bed untimely sent her.*

Or, as Broome wrote:

> *A coming storm your shooting corns presage,*
> *And aches will throb, your hollow tooth will rage.*

Dr. Jenner's dog, I do believe, had rheumatism. Before
a storm, when his pains were intense, he tried the only
remedy a dog instinctively knows, eating grass.

A drop in the barometer will affect everyone differently, but generally speaking, the effects of whiskey and the physical effects of atmospheric pressure change are alike. Both attack the blood stream in the same manner. When an air pilot gets anoxia (lack-of-pressure sickness) he may become morose, belligerent, gay or loud. He might laugh for little reason or he might weep, but he would do exactly what he would be doing if he were drunk. A change in weather is also a change in air pressure, and will usually have the effect of at least one sip of whiskey. I do my best creative work during stormy weather and I find that exactly one alcoholic drink will provide a like stimulation.

Knowing that I create and paint my best during low pressure and that things are easier to sell in high pressure, I should definitely regulate my work to the barometer readings. Everyone should, I guess.

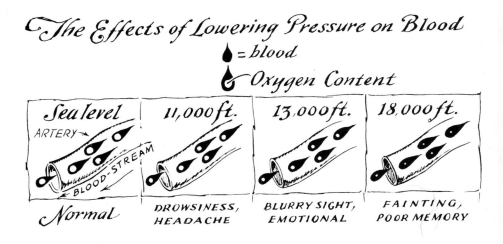

The Effects of Lowering Pressure on Blood

♦ = *blood*

🌑 *Oxygen Content*

Sea level	*11,000 ft.*	*13,000 ft.*	*18,000 ft.*
ARTERY → BLOOD-STREAM			
Normal	DROWSINESS, HEADACHE	BLURRY SIGHT, EMOTIONAL	FAINTING, POOR MEMORY

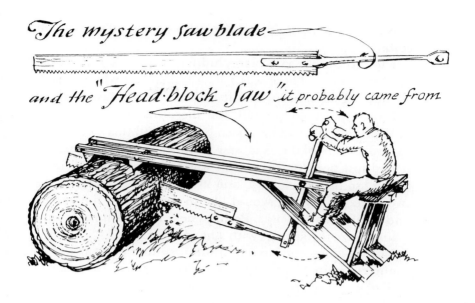

The mystery saw blade—

and the "Head-block Saw" it probably came from

I HAVE LONG FOLLOWED the practice of eating oysters only in months with the letter R in them, but I have just learned that this rule first evolved from ancient weatherlore. In regard to the making of household fires, it was said:

The chill is on from near and far
In all the months that have an R.

You might not meet as many friends that way, but the sport of chopping wood and splitting rails is as much exercise and fun as golf. The fireplaces at Weather Hill are already in use, and I find a daily chore at the woodpile is good for both spirit and waistline. There is the greatest satisfaction in striking a log in the exact spot you aim at. Besides, an ax is so typically a man's instrument. It was the first tool devised by humans, and the tradition that surrounds its exploits gives the ax a personality of its own. A saw is a cold and impersonal thing, but men collect axes as boys collect pocketknives. They enjoy the feel and lines of a well-curved ax handle as they also do a good gun or golf club.

I found an old saw blade hidden in the stone wall behind the house. There was a long forked rod where a handle should have been, and it looked like the saw from an old water-powered sawmill. But there was never a sawmill at Weather Hill, so I had been baffled until this week when I saw a picture of the exact saw blade in an 1880 newspaper. It had just been patented and was called a "sawmill head block," so the article said, and it "spelled the doom for the two man pit-saw." I would like to reconstruct the gadget and see if it really works. Perhaps next Indian summer time I can amaze the farmers with a head-block saw.

Europe does not have its Indian summer but it has its counterpart in "Saint Luke's little summer," which is a spell of unseasonably fine and dry weather, supposed to start on the eighteenth of October. It is supposed also to end on October 28, which is known as Saint Jude's Day. It invariably rains on Saint Jude's Day, and although the folklore superstition about it is untrue, it has been brought to light by modern statistics that the chance of a completely dry day in England reaches a minimum on that day, October 28.

Monday seems to have a claim toward being gloomy and rainy. This probably began from the day's being observed by housewives who had their washday interrupted by bad weather. Saturday likewise has been the fair day in superstition. The *Farmer's Almanac* by Samuel H. Wright mentions a finding of a Dr. Foster in the eighteenth century that "If the new moon falls on a Saturday, the following twenty days will be wet and windy. This," reports Dr. Foster, "has been true in nineteen cases out of twenty." This particular almanac has been one of my favorites because it starts by saying, "It is just to state to the public that they know as much about weather for the coming year as we do. No mathematician or astronomer, however able in his profession, can possibly cipher out the weather. When such predictions are seen in Almanacs, they should be regarded as mere guess work, entitled to no confidence, and as likely to fail as to be true." Hurrah for Samuel H. Wright.

This week while doing research into my old almanacs, I was startled by a blast outside, presumably from some nearby building project. But the fire warden came by the house later to ask if I knew anything about it. Several windows in the neighborhood had been cracked, and because this is forest-fire time, he was checking on blasting which might result in bush fires. The next day I learned that the blast was caused by the dive of a jet plane. What changes have come since the days of my almanacs and now!

I understand that the waves around a meteor (or shooting star) are similar to those around a plane when it causes a sonic boom. Both pile up the air in front of them faster than the air can get out of their way. Why there is no "sonic boom" accompanying a shooting star seems strange. But as it has been speeding through silent space for centuries, I

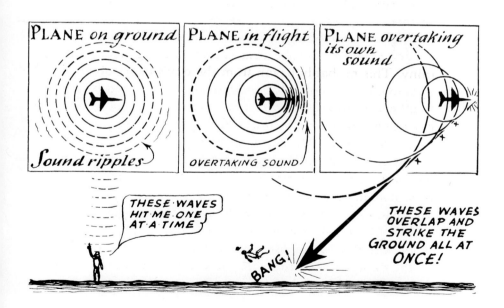

163

guess there is just no sound for it to overtake. So no boom. These meteors, which are often no bigger than a piece of dust, are not what you actually see; it is the air piled up in front of them which you see, heated into bright incandescence by friction when they strike the upper air.

The drawing, which is my attempt to explain the mechanics of a sonic boom, shows that a supersonic plane in going "faster than sound" goes faster than its own sound waves can travel ahead of it and thereby overtakes its own sound waves. At places marked X, the waves overlap themselves, causing a series of explosions which reach you as one giant roar.

Visibility   *Composition*

BLUISH-WHITE

LAYERS

HAZE

DUST FROM LAND
OR
SALT FROM SEA

MORE THAN 5/8 MI.

MIST

LESS THAN 50 FT. TO 5/8 MI.

FOG

WATER DROPLETS

Sᴏᴍᴇ ꜰᴀʀᴍᴇʀꜱ say that Indian summer ends when **First** the haze loses its blueness. Others say the season is over when autumn fogs set in. Both are right, for when the haze of In- **Week** dian summer changes to mist and fog, winter is well on its **of** way. Mist and fog are made of cloud material, but haze is composed of dust from the land and salt from the sea in **November** particles too small to be visible. It makes distant dark objects appear blue and distant white objects look yellow.

Mist is a scattered, thin formation of water droplets, irregular in outline and like a low wisp of cloud. Fog is mist that has acquired more density and well-defined edges. Pilots refer sarcastically to all three as the lowest form of cloud, but when smoke is added to the mixture (smog), you have the lowest of the low.

As I look outside, there is a layer of white over the valley floor that makes the big barns look as though they are floating in a lake. I hope this occurrence is an exception and that the season has not really changed yet.

I do believe that New England is at its best in November. The pattern of colors against the opposite hillside has become too complex to describe. Looking at it is as inspiring as beholding a sunset. Wondering if there is a rule about each tree having its definite autumn color, I set about picking out the recognizable trees on the hillside and listing them. Hitherto, I had only thought about identifying a tree from a great distance by its shape, but this idea of naming a tree by its autumn color is a new and interesting game. Here is my list for anyone who wishes to try it:

> *Yellows:* Tulip, beech, ironwood, gingko
> *Reds:* Oak, red maple, black gum
> *Oranges:* Sassafras, sugar maple, hornbeam
> *Purples:* White ash and mountain ash
> *Browns and Tans:* Oaks and hickory

Sumac has vermilion with dashes of yellow in it, and dogwood has a rich crimson all its own.

Today these colorings are nothing but added zest to our landscape, but a hundred years ago they were also our paint supply. The early farmer bought only indigo for paints and dyes; the rest were taken from the trees and berries or "raised" right along with the crops. Clothing and cloth were dyed with butternut (brown), hickory (yellow), maple (gray), sumac (red), sassafras (orange), and pokeweed (purple). So, to some extent, the autumn landscape was a gigantic palette to the housewife of early America.

Oddly enough, there is a Bureau of Standards example for almost every commodity but color. The colors of butternut, hickory, maple, and sumac could be depended on but now our complicated supply of changing paint shades is certainly confusing and unhandy. I painted the living room of Weather Hill with "Wedgewood" paint, which I was told was a new name for "Williamsburg blue." But when I ran out of paint I found it was discontinued and the same brand name offered me "Colonial blue" as the nearest shade. New colors pop up almost daily, named after a popular song, a movie, or the shade of the President's wife's new dress. The old ways were often best, for walnut dye and all the others are the same today as they were two hundred years ago.

My artist neighbor, C. E. Monroe, Jr., is painting at present a magazine cover that features an American flag; it is interesting to note that he has used more time in research toward finding the exact red in our flag than he has in doing the actual painting. He has so far bought seven flags, looked the color up in illustrated dictionaries and made a special trip to New York. The "right red," when it is printed on the cover, will probably look incorrect. I shall vote for the next office-seeker who plans to establish a Bureau of Color Standards.

One of the paint secrets of New England that has been forgotten is the habit of painting dark hallways yellow. Yellow was the color chosen by ancient religions for its mystic light-absorbing quality and the fact that it excites the least emotion.

Weather Hill has two narrow staircases which I find (under many flaked-off coats of paint) were once a bright yellow. I shall redo them in the same manner. One flight, typically New England, is made for walking up and down sideways. To add to its complexity, each step is a different height. I have memorized the heights of the steps for going up, but when I want to descend quickly I use the front stairs. The first Connecticut farmers seemed to dislike stairs, making them almost ladder-steep and then hiding them away in closets. The best stair maker was the one who could build a stair well in the least possible space.

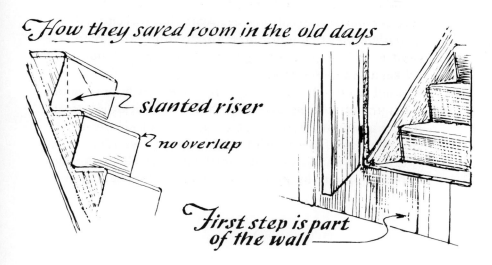

How they saved room in the old days

slanted riser

no overlap

First step is part of the wall

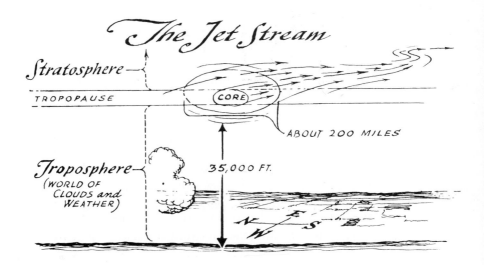

The Jet Stream

Stratosphere—

TROPOPAUSE

CORE

ABOUT 200 MILES

35,000 FT.

Troposphere—
(WORLD OF
CLOUDS and
WEATHER)

**Second
Week
of
November**

A STEADY BAROMETRIC PRESSURE, and a still calm has settled over the countryside. The poor visibility and scatterings of mist in the morning lead me to believe that a mild warm front passed during the night and left this blob of moist air behind.

When the air is so still, it is hard to believe that there are winds howling by a few miles overhead. Yet my neighbor Al Weber, who navigates for an airline, stopped by, telling me of his experience with the jet stream last night. He got home hours earlier, it seems, because he happened into the core of a particularly strong jet stream that was clocked over Philadelphia at close to three hundred miles an hour. He tried to explain what this newly found high-altitude wind is like, and I understand it is a high-speed stream of air embedded in the prevailing west-to-east wind flow at about thirty thousand feet. The main North American jet stream hovers at about fifty-five degrees north latitude during the summer and "goes south for the winter," wandering between thirty and fifty degrees north latitude. The trick seems to be not only to locate the jet stream but to locate its core, where the greatest speed occurs; if you are going in the same direction, you are in luck. If you are going in the opposite direction and your path is through it, a detour many miles around it can avoid head winds and still save time.

It is interesting how much the behavior of air is like that of water. When scientists study atmospheric phenomena they often use water to experiment with. The jet stream, I guess, is like a passage through the middle of a brook: the whole brook flows one way but there is usually a narrow ribbon of water in the middle that flows past rocks and eddies, moving faster than the rest of the water. The "white-water canoeist" who seeks to keep his craft in that middle stream is probably very much like navigator Weber, who checks on weather map isobars to keep his plane in a jet stream.

Wind is such a fascinating subject, I have often wondered why more books have not been written on it. Once I had a letter from a chimney builder in Brooklyn, ordering one of my weather books; another came from a farmer building a wind-powered well. So many people are awed and confounded by sensational writings about hurricanes and cloud seeding and the unusual antics of weather, yet feel so close to the everyday wind that dries the clothes on the line or lifts the kite into the sky.

Sometimes it takes a child to do the teaching. One once remarked to me that it looked as though the trees were exercising during a strong wind. I'd never thought about it before, but that was exactly what the trees were doing, thanks to the wind. The wind strengthens plants, and does all the things that exercise does for a human being. One of my own observations about the wind has been that animals graze with their tails to the wind. Flyers who make forced landings might observe the way cows are grazing to determine the way the wind is blowing. Virgil, in his *Georgics,* credits the cow with being very weatherwise.

> *The cow looks up [he says], and from afar can find*
> *The change of heaven, and snuffs it in the wind.*

Actually, I believe grazing animals instinctively face down-wind because an attacking animal would approach from that direction, where his scent would not be carried on ahead as a warning.

Throughout the ages, men have made more notes on the wind than on any other subject of weather. Here are a few that I have lifted from the almanacs:

> *When the wind is in the south,*
> *It blows the bait in the fishes' mouth.*

In a south wind the sea appears blue and clear; in a north wind it appears darker.—ARISTOTLE

Do business with men when the wind is from the northwest.—BENJAMIN FRANKLIN

In hot climates the wind sets from the sea to the land during the day; from the land to the sea during the night.—J. F. DANIELL

Industrial meteorologists often overlook the wind and overestimate the effects of pressure and humidity. The effect of wind will be spiritually buoyant and conducive to sales for some items, while, as in the case of the housewife who bakes at home and shops for food less during a breezy day, wind can slacken the sale of other items. One baking firm gears its output largely to the wind and saves thousands of leftover loaves from being baked.

A writing about weather vanes states that the word "news" derives from the four cardinal points of the compass: North, East, West and South. That is an interesting statement but I can find nothing to back it up with, so I shall just continue thinking of it as an interesting statement. But weatherwise, the direction of the wind is the most important news of the moment.

News and the Weather...they travel together

North wind

Snow

Leaves

Brush

Snow

Cross-section

An Indian-trail "Brush shelter"

WINTER is like a blustery visitor who comes un- **Third**
invited to track your floors with snow and leave your door
ajar to the cold, yet makes good company when the day is **Week**
done and the fireplace takes over as host. Nietzsche said it **of**
nicely in referring to winter as ". . . a bad guest that sits
with me at home; my hands are blue with his friendly **November**
handshakes."

In the country, coldness is measured not only by the thermometer but also by the wind. It is when the farmhouse
curtains move with the draft, and fireplace smoke puffs out
into the room, that cold really penetrates and makes itself
most known.

When snow has piled up around the frame farmhouse or
barn it is easier to keep it warm, for snow actually keeps
out the wind. This is the time of year that the old-time
farmer piled dried leaves and cornstalks around the base of
his barn and around the north side of his house. He probably learned this trick from the rabbits and mice that ten-
anted every snow-covered pile of cornstalks in the fields. But
the Indians knew it too; all along the trails of two hundred
years ago there were "brush shelters" that were mentioned
in early writings of cross-country travelers. George Washington often spent the night in a brush shelter during his
surveying days.

The brush shelter was simply a lean-to of sticks and dried leaves that backed against the north and during the winter gathered a roofing of snow. By building a fire on the south side, or by hanging a blanket over the opening, the traveler was assured of a comfortable place to rest during a bad snowstorm.

Weather Hill has a mixture of sticks and cornstalks and plaster called wattle and daub, which was the insulation of two hundred years ago, in some of its northern walls. Someday the insulating quality of cornstalks, dried leaves or other such vegetation will be used again for home insulation, and the most promising crop, I understand, is the common cattail. At the present time the United States has over a hundred and fifty thousand square miles of cattails that would produce thirty-four million pounds of oil and one hundred and sixty-six million pounds of cattle food. The cattail produces ten times more edible tubers per acre than potatoes, besides giving enormous amounts of fiber and fluff for heat insulation, life jackets, mattresses, wallboard, and the manufacture of paper. How odd it will be if predictions come true and the American cattail, which was once only an ornament, becomes one of our most productive farm plants.

Everyone is looking forward to a good winter and the proverbial white Christmas. The store windows feature skis and ice skates and toboggans. I have hanging among my collection of ancient tools some early ice skates, and just to see how the old-timers skated, I am going to have the screws removed (they had screws that fitted into your heel) and fit them with straps for my own use. It is not surprising to notice that like the steel in the tools, the skate blades are still sharp and unrusted.

One skate has etched into it *Fast as flying*. I had always thought that a skater went very fast—probably fifty miles an hour. But on looking up this question in a modern almanac, I find that the human body has run on dry land faster than it can skate on ice. It is the ease and gliding characteristics of skating that give the illusion of greater speed.

The best sign for good ice on the lake, so the country people say, is a late freeze rather than an early one. "If there's ice in November that will bear a duck," goes an old New England jingle, "there'll be nothing after but sludge and muck." Or as one of my almanacs puts it, "Ice in November brings mud in December."

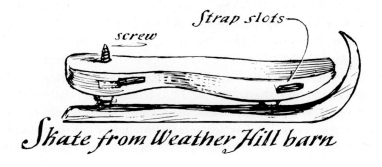

Skate from Weather Hill barn

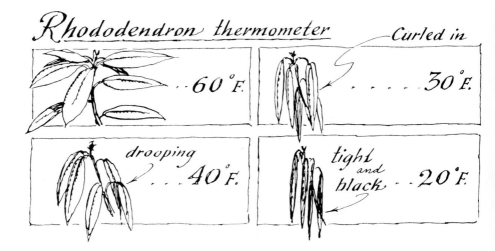

Rhododendron thermometer

Curled in

...60°F.

......30°F.

drooping
...40°F.

tight and black...20°F.

Last Week of November

THE MEDIEVAL SCHEME of seasons once dated the twenty-third of November as the beginning of winter. This day was known as Saint Clement's Day and celebrations for the inauguration of winter made it very much like Christmas today, for people used evergreens and candles and burned a great log in honor of the occasion. Whatever the weather was on this day was supposed to indicate the trend for the coming winter season. If there is anything to this year's Saint Clement's Day, the winter will be cold and dry.

No doubt about it, winter is on its way by now. The rhododendron leaves look stiff and closed, so I need not look at the thermometer: the temperature is most certainly down to freezing. The pimpernel or "poor man's weather glass" closes its petals when the humidity becomes more than eighty per cent; daisy and chickweed do the same thing. But rhododendron, known to the early American as an azalea, is the thermometer of the forest. It was said that "When wild azalea shuts its doors, that's when winter's tempest roars." A few scattered snowflakes fell this morning but only because Weather Hill is upon a hilltop: the valley

174

had none. I caught one of the flakes, and looked at it through a glass, never ceasing to wonder about the unending structural beauty that composes each snowflake.

One of my almanacs suggests the nailing of a piece of black velvet on a board to catch snowflakes; in this manner you can examine them best and they will stay frozen longer. Snowflakes, more than any other solid thing, are made in heaven. They crystallize into being while floating in the air so that their atoms, which are the building blocks of all things, have an uninterrupted ability to arrange themselves. The results surround the composition of hydrogen and oxygen in the proportion of two parts hydrogen and one part oxygen. They arrange themselves on this triangular basis as a six-faced crystal which may always be divided by six or three. Nothing on earth that I know of demonstrates the complexity yet frightening exactness of life, and includes the symbol of holiness which Trinity denotes to mankind.

I had what I thought was a powder horn hanging from the matchlock of one of my old flintlock guns. But today Jimmy the farmer took it down to look at, and blowing a note on it, set me straight. It was a cowhorn, or old hunting bugle, and not a powder horn. Nimbo, my dog, came in excitedly and expressed great interest in the musical blast. Jimmy tells me that the note carries farther to a dog's ears than the sound of a shot. He also informed me that three long blasts on a cowhorn mean "Help!" or "Come to me." Two toots are just "hello," which is answered by one toot. "Learned all that from Granddaddy," Jimmy added, "but I haven't seen a real cowhorn for many a year."

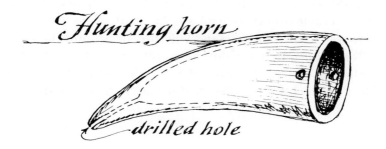

Hunting horn

drilled hole

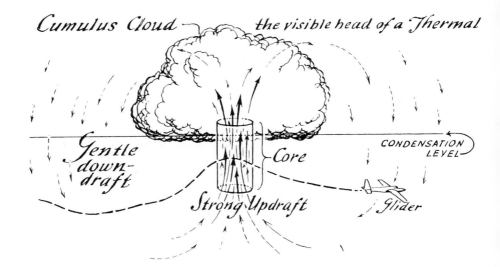

Cumulus Cloud — the visible head of a Thermal

Gentle down-draft

Core

Strong Updraft

CONDENSATION LEVEL

Glider

First Week of December A MASS of polar air came through last night and left its telltale blobs of white cumulus clouds behind. I knew the barometer had risen even before I looked at it; when I opened a bottle of mouth wash this morning, there was a soft "whoosh" of air as today's higher pressure pushed its way into the bottle where yesterday's air had been trapped. That and the refreshed way you feel when a cold mass comes through were as revealing to me as looking at a weather map.

I seldom see such big cumulus clouds without wondering whatever happened to gliding and soaring. Twenty years ago it was a growing sport but now you hear little about soaring. "Cumulus clouds," they used to teach, "are the visible heads of big thermal updrafts. Get under them and you will keep going up until you get to the top of the cloud, or the cloud begins to dissipate."

It was hard to understand why the air around the cloud falls slowly while the air in the middle goes up so fast. More air going up than coming down didn't sound logical. It wasn't until I drew a plan of the doughnutlike thermal cell for an Air Force manual that the answer got through to me. Air falls slowly all around the cell, it seems, but the same amount rushes up through a narrow chimneylike core. More air has to go through less space, so it just hurries faster.

December is no month for big cumulus clouds; I might venture to guess this will be the last day of its kind until spring. December is the farmer's account-settling month, at one time called "the Sunday of the months." From what the almanacs say, there was little to do during this month except the making of plans for the next year. Furthermore, with the coming observance of Christ's birthday, this was a month set aside for visiting folks or just resting. In the early days, when everything was made at the farm, there was no Christmas shopping to do; gift quilts, sleds, clothing, cookies, everything was ready for giving by the first of December.

One of my most remembered gifts was a rag rug made by a farmer's wife. She had just moved into the neighborhood, and the rags were really bits of all the cloth things saved from her old home and remnants from her new place. The rags in the center of the round rug looked older and faded; there were scraps of red-flannel nightgown, a few fancy ginghams from newlywed days, bits from a child's nursery and richer cloths and curtains that appeared as things began to prosper. Perhaps it was all my imagination, but I do believe the giver's first few married years were tenderly represented in this woven diary, starting from the center and working outward, where the binding finally touched my floorboards with ribbons saved from old Christmas wrappings.

I've never lost my way in Connecticut without the experience being a great pleasure. In going to the Shiver Mountain Press to pick up my Christmas cards, I made a wrong turn somewhere and spent a half hour trying to find my way out of so magnificent a countryside that it was almost a disappointment to find my way back.

There is a horseshoe curve on the way that has an interesting story. It seems a particularly unfriendly Indian named Big Fox and his family had an encampment thereabouts. Even long after Big Fox had disappeared, travelers gave a wide berth to the place, and the circled trail was never straightened out. It went from footpath to wagon trail and finally to automobile road, still avoiding the memory of unfriendly Big Fox. I suppose many established roads are built on the paths made by trappers, Indians, or even wild beasts.

The spirit of Yankee peddling is not dead. A farmer in the valley is selling tinseled yule logs for artificial fireplaces in the city. He says he can't understand why anyone would buy them but some city fellow has been selling almost all the big birch logs he can prepare.

I have yet to see a yule log burned, and don't know how it would differ from any other log that burns in my fireplace. But I do know that "yule" originally had nothing to do with Christmas except that they both occurred about the same time. It was the name given to Midwinter Feast, which celebrated the season of winter. The ceremony of the yule log was actually in honor of the god of storm, and bits of the charred Yule Day log were distributed and kept within houses to protect them from lightning and wind during the coming year. So the Happy Yuletide of Christmas-card fame approaches the spirit of our present-day season in a very roundabout way.

Although Christmas cards are traditional, the custom is comparatively new, even less than a hundred years old. The first cards in America were engraved by Louis Prang in 1874 for export to England. They did so well that they were introduced in America in 1875. Christmas seals are even more recent, being designed by Emily Bissell of Wilmington in 1907. In the earlier days, Christmas mail was limited by high postal rates. Letters were all made on one piece of paper and each extra page became an extra postal rate. Envelopes were introduced in 1839 and were first called "paper-en-velopers." It is often difficult to believe that so many things we take for granted now are all products of this past busy century. A recent TV program showed young Lincoln wait-ing on a customer in a store, putting groceries in a bag. But the paper bag was unheard of until 1867 and machine-made bags were not patented until 1872, seven years after Lincoln died.

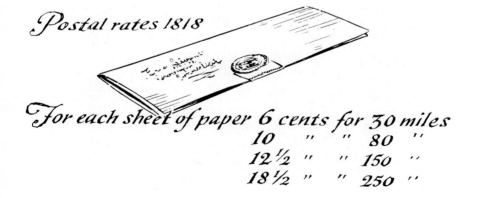

Postal rates 1818

For each sheet of paper 6 cents for 30 miles
10   "   "   80   "
12½   "   "   150   "
18½   "   "   250   "

"Snow shadows"

Second Week of December During THE NIGHT a light snow fell, which the morning sun melted away. But going to town very early, I noticed that the cedars on the hills all had "white shadows" where the sun had not yet reached. This is an effect I have often seen while flying: when a light snow is disappearing before the morning sun's rays, you may see the outlines of buildings and trees laid out on the ground in snow, like an architectural drawing.

It is odd how the sun's rays can melt away snow when the sun is shining from the horizon, while often snow will persist in patches even when the sun is directly overhead. The very whiteness of snow protects it against the midday sun, because white reflects the rays back without absorbing the heat. This explains why city snow, which is so often less white because of soot and traffic dirt, melts quicker than snow on country roads and hills. It simply absorbs more heat.

Going to town this Sunday morning, I passed a farm stand where Christmas greens were left standing out on display. A great flock of birds had descended on the holly and were denuding it of the red berries. Actually the berries were fulfilling one of the purposes that they were created for. Yet I believe that I was more amused than the stand owner must have been when he found his berryless holly.

The use of holly as a Christ-symbol is older by far than the Christmas tree, being adopted by the early Roman Christians. A holly-decorated Christmas scroll dated 1450 has been found in England. But although holly now symbolizes Christ's birth, it first represented the Crucifixion instead. The legend is that Christ's crown of dead thorns miraculously sprouted into life, green appearing from between the thorn-points while the drops of His blood became the red berries. There are hill people in the Southern states who still carry on Elizabethan reference to "holy berries" rather than holly berries. So the holly symbol, which had to do with the Crucifixion, was originally an Easter decoration.

One of my oldest almanacs tells how holly leaves were used at that time by the Indians to brew tea and make an edible mash, while only this week I read that according to George W. Cavanaugh of Cornell University, the holly leaf might prove to be America's first food of tomorrow. "Holly's fat content," says the report, "might be doubled by breeding, but at present its analysis, compared with popular grains, is most remarkable." I quote from the *Rural New Yorker:*

	Proteins Per cent	Fat Per cent
Holly Leaf	14.56	13.56
Oats	11.8	5.0
Barley	12.4	1.8
Wheat	12.0	2.0
Corn	10.5	5.0
Rye	10.5	1.7

There are still roadside stands in New England that are not open on Sunday. It seems only yesterday that it was against the law to operate a business on the Sabbath. But it is often the law itself that defeats the purpose, for when a punishment is threatened, the purpose is weakened. "Respect for the Sabbath," as Benjamin Franklin put it, "must come from within one's self." One of the leftovers from New England's Sabbath laws is the superstition that it is illegal to write a check on Sunday, or that the check will be valueless. The bank is holding your money on Sundays and making as much money from it as it does on weekdays, so Sunday checks are as good as gold.

One of my inspirations for collecting these notes has been a diary of 1850, but I had read it nearly through without noticing that all Sunday entries had been skipped. Indeed the Sabbath in those days was held rigidly, even in one's diary. On further observation through my almanacs, I find that even the overland stages observed the Sabbath, and all business truly stood still.

The Connecticut Statutes of 1830 (Title 84, Section 7) reads: "No proprietor or driver of any coach, waggon, sleigh . . . shall suffer or allow any person to travel except from necessity or charity on the Lord's day, or penalty of twenty dollars for each offense."

Twenty dollars in 1830 was a large sum: I found report of only one Connecticut stage line that paid it, so the law seems to have been well respected. It also deemed "any traveller, drover, waggoner or teamster who travelled abroad on the Lord's day . . . liable to a fine of four dollars."

Until recently, and still in many cases, covered-bridge tolls were not exacted from churchgoers. The same went for toll turnpikes, and the Sabbath rule was put into state turnpike laws. Frequently when a church was just the other side of a covered bridge, the toll-taker simply hung out a small white board on which there was painted a cross, which meant "free passage to churchgoers." Very often the board on which the bridge tolls were marked had the cross painted on its back, and on Sundays the board was simply reversed. There were also cases where Sunday tolls were collected but donated to the local church. Neighbor Wanzer commented that it would be nice if the George Washington Bridge would do just that each Sunday. Amen to that thought.

Sabbath Greeting

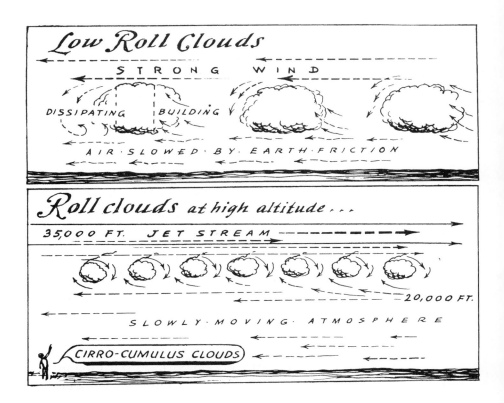

Low Roll Clouds

STRONG WIND

DISSIPATING | BUILDING

AIR · SLOWED · BY · EARTH · FRICTION

Roll clouds at high altitude...

35,000 FT. JET STREAM

—20,000 FT.

SLOWLY · MOVING · ATMOSPHERE

CIRRO-CUMULUS CLOUDS

**Third
Week
of
December**

Oㅏ NE OF THE THINGS I have never seen in a meteorological textbook is how to tell the direction of the upper wind according to the formation of clouds there. Generally speaking, clouds roll up at a right angle to (or "against") the wind, but frequently you will see a plume of cloudform (usually cirrus) flowing with the wind.

Flyers now say they sometimes spot jet-stream flows of stronger wind by the appearance of rolls of high cirro-cumulus or "mackerel clouds." The theory of this is that low-altitude wind might be slower or even moving in the opposite direction to a high air stream, and clouds are "rolled" as you would roll a pencil between your two palms going in opposite directions. Overhead this morning, I saw a fine mass of these mackerel clouds at a right angle to the west, while the ground wind was from the south. Perhaps I was looking at a jet stream. Cirro-cumulus is not generally regarded as a roll cloud because it is so high. The effect is more like ripples than rolls and the whole pattern resembles fine rippled sand.

Roll clouds often seem to be blowing with the wind, although they are constantly being born and dissipated as they "move" along. As fast as the lee side disappears, the windward side builds up again, so the illusion is that the clouds stay whole and move very slowly with the breeze.

I worked this week on a cloud mural for an airport dedicated to a flyer who was killed in the air. Clouds, sky and sunbeams seem unusually suited to religious messages. Angels and heavenly apparitions are mythical and archaic unto this logical age, but because of the fact that "heaven" is supposed to be "up there" or any direction away from the earth's center, the sky becomes an ideal subject for church decoration.

There seems to be a great trend away from tradition in church architecture. Churches that look like automobile showrooms, with modernistic stained-glass windows, are appearing all over New England. "Unlike the story-telling windows of bygone days," says *Life*, "the best stained glass that is being produced today is semi- or completely abstract."

I guess there's no law saying a church must look like a church, but I've often wondered what confusion there would be if the Maker were also an abstractionist and He made things look like what they aren't. The abstractionist has the right to his opinions, according to my way of thinking, but the architecture of religion should embody tradition and deplore the abstract.* From the mountain to the snowflake, the

* According to Webster, theological tradition is "Among Christians, that body of doctrine and discipline, or any article thereof, put forth or revealed by Christ or his apostles, and not committed to writing."

molecule, and finally down to the atom, there is nothing abstract about the orderliness of life.

My idea of a perfect church window is not the usual "jukebox maze" of stained-glass colors, but the clearest and biggest pane of glass looking toward open sky. Lincoln said he could not imagine a person looking at the sky and denying a God; I agree with him that clouds and sky are the perfect backdrop for peace, solace and the contemplation of life. An architect criticized my placing of a picture window in the front face of Weather Hill, but the panorama of seasons and the ever-changing parade of skies that I can now see from my living room are more important to me than even television.

Early church windows were often pieced and leaded for no other reason than that large pieces of glass were hard to get. In Europe, the first windows were without glass and were called "wind eyes" instead of windows. In America, the first windows were small and were the movable property of every house owner. When you moved, you took your windows along with you.

an Early "Wind Eye" →
had a baffle to keep the
wind out.

Wall

Wind

"December's last week the Animals speak"

—NEW ENGLAND FOLKLORE

I FIND MYSELF surrounded by old almanacs and the notes that I have been scribbling on the backs of my barograph charts for an entire year. It has been a pleasure keeping such an account, and I must say that it has been a means of learning something new every day. When you observe even the simplest things of everyday life, there is always another question to be answered; and often the farthest-reaching discoveries have come from providing new questions rather than new answers.

Last Week of December

My barograph is doing a fine job of being a base for a basket of Christmas greens. Its tireless pen has breathed up and down with the weight of many mountains of air, and it has recorded the profiles of good weather and bad.

The farther back my almanacs go, the less Christmas celebration there seemed to be; solemnity was the note in those days. The first Christmas at Plymouth was purposely spent at hard labor, because the Pilgrims scorned Christmas as a human invention. No one was a true Christian, they argued, until he ceased celebrating Christmas and Easter. Later, it was even considered a crime to celebrate those days.

The mantel at Weather Hill has several nail holes where I like to think homemade woolen stockings once hung on Christmas Eve. Some of the holes are square from ancient hand-cut nails; others are smaller and recent, made by thumbtacks. The meaning of Christmas is often lost in the city, where Christmas is celebrated by buying; but while there are fireplaces to warm the soul and souls that can be warmed, the true spirit will always live around the hearth.

I wonder what other Christmases in this house have been like. I am sure there was the smell of pine and bayberry, of mince pies and cooking, and the stamping of feet at the door as visitors left their sleds and kicked snow away from their boots.

My Christmas tree is ordered—a live one in a pot. I shall not only plant it outside later on, but try what one of my almanacs suggests, to dip popcorn in hot molasses and shower the branches with it. The cold is supposed to harden the molasses and fasten the kernels to the tree so the birds may have a fine feeding station.

A neighbor's child, who was surprised that "Jesus was born on the same day as Christmas," asked why we don't call it "Christ's Birthday," the same as we do for George Washington and Abraham Lincoln. Every year I grope for an appropriate idea for my Christmas card; I think next year I shall use the greeting, *"Joyous Christ's Birthday."*

Outside, the hollowness of prestorm atmosphere has changed to the sound-deadening effect of snowfall. The air is unmoving and snowflakes fall slowly. My dog Nimbo, snug by the fireplace, shows the white of an opened eye as he observes the soft whistle and snap of a burning green log. Another year has been completed and all is well at Weather Hill. A joyous Christ's Birthday to everyone!

The End...

...as we look back, is also the Beginning

Folklore of American Weather

by
ERIC SLOANE

To Ruth, the setter of my barograph and chief tester of my weather folklore. Champion of honesty and exactness, she gave this book her stalwart help, without which it would have been finished a darn sight sooner.

Author's note.

Folklore can be a very loose word, used to cover a lack of knowledge of the very thing that folklore means. When there is nothing else to attribute a hearsay belief to, it so often becomes branded as genuine folklore. I recall hearing about an early inn known as The Bag of Nails, which was supposed to have been named Bag-o'-nails Inn many years ago. Folklore had contrived many tales about the early hand-made-nail makers and how they used to "pay off their inn bills by exchanging bags of nails." Yet after research it was found that the inn was first called The Bacchanalian. The farmers had found that name a bit too difficult, and it was probably by purposeful mispronunciation that it became called the Bag-o'-nails. The final inn sign displayed a cloth bag with nails in it!

Another time, when I was writing about early-American weathervanes, I related, tongue-in-cheek, an old Maine story of how down east they used to hang a heavy chain on a tall pole. "When that chain stood straight out," the story goes, "the old-timers knew there was a wind a-blowin'." You can imagine my amazement when later I found an article written on weathervanes that had taken my story seriously: There was even a drawing of the "Maine chain-weathervane"!

Another time, when I was writing of old covered bridges, I told how the horses *clobbered* through the inner bridge, making the floor boards rattle. But the proofreader overlooked my misspelling when I wrote *cloobered* instead of *clobbered*! And since that time I have seen several references to "horses cloobering through the old covered bridges," and I guess the strange word *cloober* might have become part of covered-bridge folklore. And so it goes. There are many things passed off as folklore that were plain mistakes or the invention of some agile mind.

Therefore, in collecting a group of American weather sayings, I have made a special effort to track them down and to separate the true from the false. Our time is already so poor in lore, and there are so many valuable bits of weather information, that to mix the true with jackass jingles and silly superstition would be sad indeed.

The last part of this small book is in the form of an alphabetical folklore dictionary so that you may look up signs involving stars, wind, dew, or whatever else you might wish. Following each saying you will find a **T** (true), **F** (false), or **P** (possible). Each saying is printed in italics while the comments or explanations are printed below in roman type. You might find some disagreement with my comments, but I have simply done my best to research each saying, and the opinions are entirely my own. Many sayings have become popular entirely by word-of-mouth; if you can add any to my list, do send them in to me so that a future edition of this book might be so enriched.

Because I believe the sky was made for beholding and that any weather-wise person enjoys a fuller and more enjoyable life, I recommend to you the poetry and lore of weather.

Eric Sloane

Weather Hill Farm
Cornwall Bridge
Connecticut

The Beginning

About half of all the American weather books start out with "that famous Mark Twain saying" that "everyone talks about the weather, but nobody does anything about it." Actually this was not a Twainism at all, but was said by a man named C. D. Warner. Twain quoted Warner in a speech, and the saying became known as one of Mark Twain's from that time on. Twain did, however, say, "If you don't like the weather in New England, just wait a few minutes," and that proverb is most typical of American weather talk. Benjamin Franklin, who said, "Some are weatherwise, some are otherwise," also said, "Know the signs of the sky and you will far the happier be." There seems to be something typically rural American about weather observance: here, instead of *hello*, one most often nods and says, "Nice day today." It has been said that the average American can't start a conversation without referring to the weather first. It is natural, then, that there should also be a good store of American weather folklore.

Being aware that most early-American customs were brought intact from overseas, a student of folklore might wonder how much genuine American folklore there can be. To answer this, I quote from a letter written in 1762 from a father to his son who was preparing a trip to these shores.

"The greatest differences here," he wrote, "you shall find in the weather. You shall need the stoutest of cloathing. The sky and its signs and the seasonal changes are most unlike those to which we are accustomed."

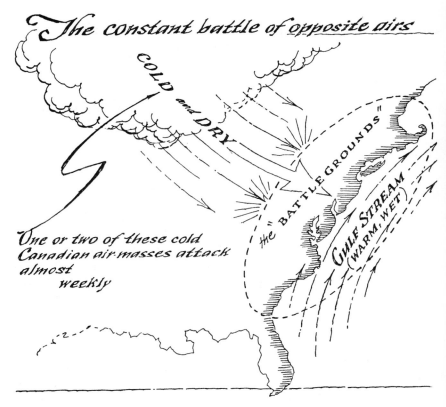

The constant battle of opposite airs

COLD and DRY

the "BATTLE GROUNDS"

GULF STREAM (WARM, WET)

One or two of these cold
Canadian air masses attack
almost
weekly

The American Atlantic coast's *mean* climate is somewhat like that of England or Europe, yet the local sudden weather changes and the resulting inability to predict them made farm life most difficult during the earliest pioneer days. Most of the weather lore that they had already learned overseas did not seem to apply to the New World.

Nowhere on earth are there greater variations in temperature or suddenness of change than in America. New England's climate, for example, ranges from 110 degrees in summer to minus 55 degrees in winter. Our floods occur in all seasons, our droughts are severe. Hurricanes born over fifteen hundred miles away in the tropics seem to reach New England without any loss of

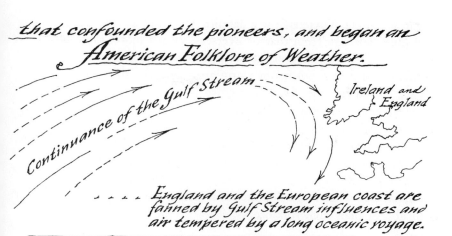

that confounded the pioneers, and began an American Folklore of Weather.

Continuance of the Gulf Stream

Ireland and England

England and the European coast are fanned by Gulf Stream influences and air tempered by a long oceanic voyage.

power, sometimes even picking up some punch along the way. Therefore when the pioneer reached our shores, he found climatic conditions so severe that crops or even lives were lost because of the inability to predict weather.

The warm Gulf Stream that tempers the moist climate of the British Isles is strongest off our own Atlantic coast; its effects make our shore line one of mild climate. Yet blobs of cold, dry Canadian air attack this shore-line atmosphere of warmth and wetness on an average of once a week. The clash usually occurs from five to over fifty miles inland, and the results are quick drops in temperature, towering storm clouds, and sudden precipitation.

The variation in our land contours added another note of uncertainty, which further detracted from the pioneer's ability to predict American weather. It might rain hard in some valley of New York State, while the adjacent high ground only a mile away would miss the storm entirely. Or a Massachusetts sea cove might be enveloped in fog and rain while an arm of land a mile away would be in complete sunshine. This sort of thing seldom happens in England.

Over a period of about a century, then, after each area had devised its own lists of weather signs, a native American folklore began to evolve. There is now a definite American weather folk-lore quite separate from that of overseas; what's more, there is still need of it. Our weather bureau can foretell what is over the horizon, and it can spot major storm areas and plot their movements, but when the weather picture is at all uncertain, the experts cannot say for sure what the weather will be in any specific locality.

The national weather map over 50 per cent of the time is an uncertain picture; local radio broadcasts give such phrases as "three out of ten chances" or "scattered showers" in their predictions. Yet what more definite information can be given for a local area than such folklore as:

> *When Lookout Mountain [Tennessee] has its cap on, it will rain in six hours.* •

> *When you can see the Connecticut shore [from Long Island] with great clarity, it will rain in about twelve to fifteen hours.* •

> *Fog from seaward in Maine, don't expect the rain:*
> *Fog from land in warm, batten down for storm.*
>
> •

> *When wild geese fly to the southeast in Kansas, expect a blizzard.* •

> *Except in winter, a north wind over inland New York and New Jersey brings two full days of drear and drizzle.*
>
> •

And so the old-timer can often look overhead, sniff the breeze or look at the sky, and give you a pin-point forecast that no government weatherman would dare risk.

Often you can separate the American folklore from the European by observing a blunt American "Will it or will it not rain?" attitude typical of American practicality. In Britain, where most people go around carrying an umbrella as they might a cane, weather is a thing to live with, and, "Life goes on, rain or not." Of course, life in the United States goes on "rain or not" too, but our meteorological attitude seems to hinge more upon the possibilities of rain than on anything else. We think the British press a bit poetical in its observance of the sky, the clouds, or the sunset each day; on the other hand, our press is always alive with some scheme for man to "conquer the weather."

I once created a series of newspaper articles with drawings about weather, cloud observance, and folklore. I was prompted to do so when a noted publisher remarked that the most important news in any daily paper could well be the weather forecast. Yet the series was turned down by the syndicates, each of whom remarked that the American public does not want to learn about weather or to read folklore; it just wants to know whether it will rain tomorrow.

I found a pleasant reminder of the European attitude toward weather in an "almanack" poem of 1735; the sentiments there have not changed throughout the years.

> *Be not anxious, friend,*
> *About tomorrow's weather;*
> *Whether our sports it may commend,*
> *And the fair morn*
> *Deserve the tribute of the cheerful horn;*
> *Or drizzly wet compel us to sit*
> *Around the fire together, both Whigs and Tories,*
> *And ply the glass,*
> *Or, time to pass,*
> *Hum tunes and tell old stories.*

The true rural love of weather in America, along with its richness of folklore, seems to have diminished with the passing of individual farming. Farming has become a big business with little place for folklore, but a century ago farming was a way of life, a philosophy of living, rich with lore of the land.

The Almanacks

Asked to describe the old-time "almanacks" in one word, we might first strike on the word *quaint*. Yet one could call the old almanac about as quaint as we could call a modern dictionary quaint. What with the mentions of moonlore and weather prophecy, you might also think of the word *mystic*. Yet the almanac was as scientific a piece of literature as one could find for its time; it was a calendar based upon moon positions (just as our modern calendar is) with weather indications that had been tallied and averaged over a period of many years (just as our present-day long-range weather forecasts are made). The almanacs were not things collected by a few and ignored by others; they were stock tools of the day, necessary for the carrying-on of any business or even the daily routine of early-American life.

If your clock stopped and your nearest neighbor was ten miles away, you would not carry your clock with its wooden works to his place to set it, for the jiggling would upset its delicate mechanism. Instead you would watch for the sunrise or sunset or moonrise; then, by referring to your current almanac, you would know not only the date, but you could set your clock to the correct second. The tides or the position of the moon means very little to the average person today, yet in the days when there were no electric lights and much of the farming was done in moonlight, you might well have looked forward to the right moonlit night before you planned to harvest this or that field, or to make an overnight ox-cart journey.

Yes, it does seem odd to many now, that the old-timer took his almanac so seriously. Yet he would be astonished at the baseball news and TV commercials and other contemporary trivia that manage to take up so many precious hours of our lives today.

The early, soft-dirt roads of America were completely useless in or after a heavy rainfall. You gave great thought to what day you might choose to go to town, because wheels didn't turn in the old-time-road mud, and you might find yourself stranded for a day or two only a few miles away from home. In fact the roads were so impassable during wet weather that all heavy loads such as lumber or stone were saved till winter and moved by sled over the snow. The almanac was as useful for traveling as the railroad timetable is nowadays.

You might argue that almanacs were for farmers, that the lawyer or shoemaker or storekeeper need not use them. Yet the lawyer, the shoemaker, the storekeeper had to be a farmer also, for he grew his own food and fed his own horses from his own hay-field. Thus everyone in early America was close to the ways of nature, by necessity. People noticed how birds and animals built their homes each year; then they tried to compare these changes with climatic changes in order to benefit from the weather instincts of wild life. For example, in 1733 *Poor Robin's Almanack* said:

> *Observe which way the hedgehog builds her nest,*
> *To front the north or south or east or west;*
> *For if 'tis true what common people say,*
> *The wind will blow the quite contrary way.*
>
> *If by some secret art the hedgehog knows*
> *So long before, the way in which the winds will blow,*
> *She has an art which many a person lacks*
> *That thinks himself fit to make our almanacks.*

We owe many of our weather rhymes to the almanac makers, and although some of these do not actually predict weather, they do add to the richness of weather lore. Here are a few of these meteorological gems:

When it rains while the sun shines, the devil is beating his wife.
He is laughing while his wife is crying.—NEW ENGLAND.

•

The lightning is a yaller gal who lives up in the cloud.
The thunder is a black man that hollers out loud.
The black man kisses the yaller gal and thinks he is a wonder,
He bumps his head against the clouds and that's what makes
the thunder.—VIRGINIA.

•

It's raining, it's pouring, the old man's snoring [thunder].

•

When it snows, the old woman is plucking her white geese.
—MAINE.

•

When the moon wears a halo around her head, she will cry
before morning and the tears [rain] will reach you tomor-
row.—AMERICAN INDIAN.

•

It is raining cats and dogs!—PENNSYLVANIA.

This is believed to be a German mispronunciation of "cats and
ducks." The Pennsylvanian German people used to say, "It is
raining to keep in the cats and bring out the ducks." They also
said, "It is snowing for cats and ducks," which meant that the
snowfall was sufficient to track a cat or a duck through it.

•

When it thunders, the mountain men are bowling.

This is a New York State saying credited to the story of Rip
Van Winkle, although the saying is really older than Irving's

story, and he created his "little men who bowled and made thunderous noise" from this old weather saying.

•

There's news in the wind!

From Boston's *Weatherwise Almanack* of the middle 1700's, this saying was prompted from the weathervane, which has letters for north, east, south, and west, all of which happen to spell out N-E-W-S.

Weather Instruments

It has been said that except for electrical communications instruments such as telephones, TV, radio, or radar, many modern weather stations have about the same kinds of instruments as the ones Benjamin Franklin had in his laboratory. He had the anemometer, barometer, hygrometer, and such instruments as are presently used for measuring the qualities and pressures of the atmosphere. Except for the seagoing man, however, who had his barometer, or "weatherglass," few men had instruments at home with which to measure the weather. Yet all around the country there were natural instruments that told of the weather, sending out messages by smell or sound or movement and adding to the weather wisdom of the day. "The sounds and smells and signs of weather," said one almanac, "do set the full rich stage for each day of farming life."

The massive beams of ancient barns shrank or swelled with each rise or fall of the barometer and with changes of atmospheric moisture and sent out messages proclaiming a weather change. The barn builders used wooden pins, or "trunnels" (treenails), to fasten house framework together so that this fastening device could react along with the main members and not split them at the joints. The creak and groan of building timbers throughout a stormy night seldom worried the early American, for he knew that everything was working according to plan in his house framework. But he did know that the nature of the atmosphere was changing. Furniture, too, was designed to "breathe" with the weather; a simple chair might have as many as eight kinds of wood, each planned to react against the other and keep the joints tight. Thus even the cracking of furniture was understood by the weather-wise people of yesterday.

> *Hark how the chairs and tables crack!*
> *Old Betty's nerves are on the rack.*
> *...'Twill surely rain; I see with sorrow,*
> *Our jaunt must be put off tomorrow.*
> —DR. EDWARD JENNER

Any countryman will tell you that you can "hear the weather," that according to atmospheric changes, sound can differ from time to time. On the approach of a storm, the sound-dissipating irregularities of the atmosphere decrease, and sounds come to your ear with a peculiar clarity. As the Tennessee-mountain man says, "*You can hear rain in the air.*"

The many sounds of storm are of a subtle and distant lore; perhaps one of the first references is Elijah's "There is a sound of abundance of rain." The American almanacs often mentioned:

> *When the forest murmurs and the mountain roars,*
> *Then close your windows and shut your doors.*

The mention of "forest murmur" and "mountain roar" is typical of the countryman's keen notice of weather phenomena, for a cold-front storm does do just that. Wind starts from higher altitudes and then descends to earth; when a storm approaches, the flat forest simply stirs with a changed air current while the mountain tops (already in the new wind current) have begun to roar.

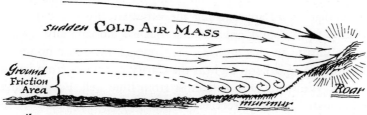

".. when the forest murmurs and the mountain roars."

205

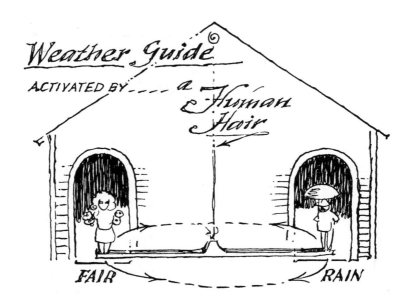

Much folklore has evolved with the habit of farming people gathering about the fireplace at night, where the sounds of the outside world come into the room by way of the chimney with extraordinary clarity. The bark of a dog, for example, or the hoot of a distant owl, can often be heard from the hearthside while such sounds may be out of earshot from outside.

Perhaps it is the heat of the chimney that causes a rapid circulation of air, which involves a sharper acoustical property. Some say that it is the loftiness of the chimney top over the various ground-level sounds of wind in the grass and the murmur of lower bushes and trees that bring in distant sounds. Others claim that sound approaching the ear vertically has a different quality from sound approaching the ear horizontally (which seems untrue to this author). Yet one of the most noticeable phenomena of balloon flight is the clarity of sounds from below. Connie Wolf, the lady balloonist from Blue Bell, Pennsylvania, is fascinated by this effect. "The little sounds from below," she says, "such as the conversation between people, the bark of a

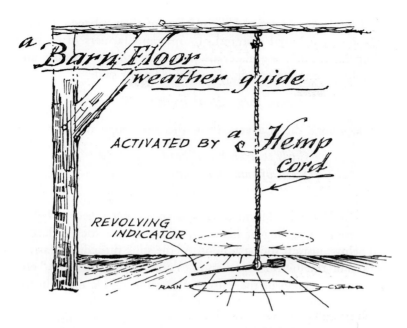

a Barn Floor weather guide

ACTIVATED BY *a Hemp cord*

REVOLVING INDICATOR

RAIN CLEAR

dog or the closing of a door, come up to the balloon as if they were only a few yards away!"

The chimney-and-hearth, then, was one of the best-known instruments of weather folklore, either by its sounds, by the way wood burned, by the formation of soot, or by the action of its smoke. People used to say:

A storm makes its first announcement down the chimney.

•

A storm wind settles in the chimney, but a clear wind coaxes out the smoke.

•

One of the farmer's weather instruments was a lump of hemp that was kept in circulating air and made a good hygrometer, or device for recording the water content of the atmosphere. The Indian used a human scalp, and the seaman used a bunch of seaweed; many farmers noted the softness of their tobacco. Fishermen sometimes used a strand of rope, and farmers often used baling cord. All these materials were affected by moisture and foretold the coming of rain. The Maine farmer said:

When ropes twist, forget your haying. **T**

The sailor's ditty, a version of the same rope weather sign, went:

Curls that kink and cords that bind
Signs of rain and heavy wind. **T**

•

The New England farmer was known to hang a piece of baling cord from the ceiling of his barn, with a heavy stick indicator tied below, just off the barn floor. As the stick turned, the farmer marked on the floor, indications of "rain," "wind," or "dry," etc. This was a version of the European weather guide made in the form of a tiny house with two doors, from which emerged either a boy or a girl, according to the weather promise. This machine used strands of human hair (blond hair reacted best), and the wetness or dryness of the hair caused the figures to swing in and out of the doors.

In England and Europe wind changes are less abrupt and less frequent than they are in the New England section of America. And as our weather may be foretold better by noticing wind direction and change than by any other method of observation, the weathervane became the nerve center for every early-American farmer's weather wisdom. Yet these first weathervanes were not like the ones we are now familiar with—the big metal rooster or whale or trotting horse, which were more for decoration than for accurate weather-lore use, some of them being so heavy that only a strong wind would budge them. The first vanes were made of light pine or cedar and made to swing with the slightest movement of air. Because no one knew the directions of east, west, north, and south better than the pioneer farmer did, there were no markers included for this purpose.

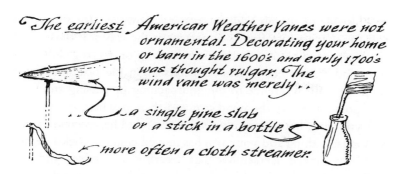

The earliest American Weather Vanes were not ornamental. Decorating your home or barn in the 1600's and early 1700's was thought vulgar. The wind vane was merely . . a single pine slab or a stick in a bottle ⸻ more often a cloth streamer.

As these old vanes were not ornamental, but were made of fragile wood, there are now none left (as far as this author knows), but only from writings can they be reconstructed in the imagination. There are all too few weathervane sayings remembered from the early days, but some of the nineteenth-century farm diaries refer to wind direction in such rhymes as:

> *A weathercock that swings to the west,*
> *Proclaims the weather to be the best.*
> *A weathercock that swings to the east,*
> *Proclaims no good to man or beast.*

What this tries to say is that any wind from southwest and around the compass to northwest does usually bring dry weather; the easterly quadrant usually brings rain.

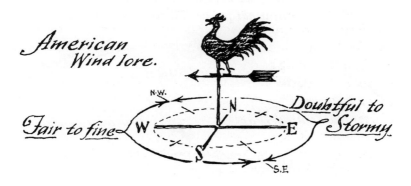

American Wind lore. *N.W.* *Fair to fine* *W* *N* *E* *Doubtful to Stormy* *S* *S.E.*

This rule of thumb is all too general, however, for the *way a wind is changing* is often as important as the way it is blowing at the moment. That is, whether it is *backing* or *veering*. Whether the wind "backs" or "veers" depends upon the position of the observer with reference to the approaching or passing storm. If you point at where the wind *was* and then at where the wind *is* and your arm has moved *clockwise*, the wind has *veered*. If you do the same thing and your arm has moved counterclockwise, the wind has *backed*. Remember that *"veering is clearing"* and you will be able to predict by this method: a backing wind brings rain. (These sayings refer to storms of a southerly direction.)

> *A veering wind will clear the sky;*
> *A backing wind says storms are nigh.*   **T**

Another weathervane saying runs:

> *Winds that swing against the sun,*
> *And winds that bring the rain are one.*
> *Winds that swing round with the sun,*
> *Keep the rain storm on the run.*   **T**

This means that a wind that changes in the direction of the sun's movement (from east to west) brings clearing; wind that changes against the sun's movement (blowing from west to east) brings storm and rain. This same rule is referred to in:

> *If the wind back against the sun,*
> *Trust it not for back it will run.*   **T**

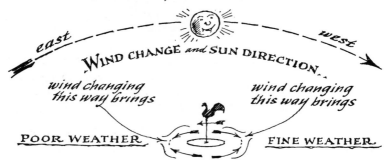

east   WIND CHANGE *and* SUN DIRECTION   west

wind changing this way brings

wind changing this way brings

POOR WEATHER

FINE WEATHER

210

The early weathervanes were often only a strip of cloth that waved from a pole. They were called wind-flags. In fact the word *vane* comes from the Anglo-Saxon *fane*, which means flag.

It is strange how little the early Americans used barometers for observing the weather, while during the early 1800's these devices had become a popular wall decoration in English homes. Only the Cape Cod weatherglass seems to be America's contribution to barometrical research and design. This object is a glass container that holds water; contact with the outside air is shut off by means of a gooseneck of glass that contains water in contact with the outside air. The battle of pressure differences between the outside air and the inside air causes the water to rise or lower accordingly. *"When the glass spills over, so will the clouds in a little while,"* goes the old Cape Cod saying.

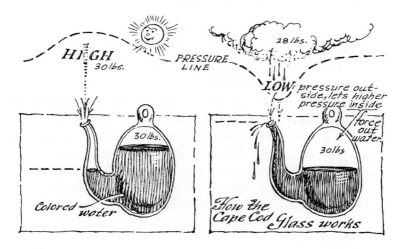

And so the sounds and actions of nature during temperature and humidity changes, along with the few weather devices that could be made around the farm, were about all that the early farmer had to combat the inconsistencies of American weather. A few people thought they could foretell weather by a special power; others could *"feel it in their bones."* As a matter of fact you *can* feel weather in your bones if your bones are extremely sensitive; old wounds and scar tissue react in the same way. Dr. Jenner wrote of such effects of weather changes:

> *"Her corns with shooting pains torment her*
> *And to her bed untimely sent her."*

And Broome said:

> *"A coming storm your shooting corns presage*
> *And aches will throb, your hollow tooth will rage."*

Actually the lowering of pressure during a coming storm is usually not enough to make a noted effect upon a normal, healthy person, but the lowering pressure plus increased humidity is what does the trick. The same stands true for temperature changes, for high heat or coldness is quite bearable to the human body, providing it is *dry*. Damp coldness or damp heat has an instant effect upon us.

In the early days of America, when the countryside was very lush with peat and moss, undrained ditches, and extensive swamps, the country atmosphere was more humid than it is now, and weather changes must have had a greater effect upon the people than they do today. Even in the mid 1700's and for the next century, when people built close to rivers to be near water-powered mills and canals, the effect of water must have made life quite different from that of today. If it were not for our countryside being doomed to disappearance, we might someday evolve a folklore of a drier or waterless living. But along with the vanishing landscape of America, folklore will someday be completely a thing of the past.

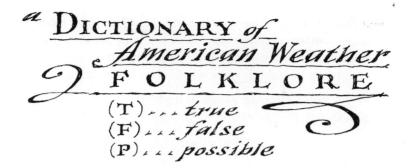

A DICTIONARY of American Weather FOLKLORE

(T)...true
(F)...false
(P)...possible

ANTS

When ants travel in a straight line, expect rain; when they scatter, expect fair weather. **F**

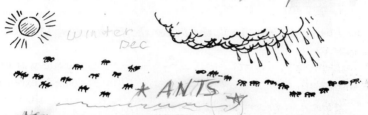

There seems to be no reason for this to be true, although many people still use it as a weather sign. In the Ozarks they say, "*Bugs march when the rain is near,*" and in Maine there is a saying, "*Flies scatter in good weather.*" The saying that "*a straight line of ants brings on a rain*" is possibly a combination of those two sayings.

•

APPLES

A tough apple skin means a hard winter. **P**

Nature does seem to be able to predict weather, and the strengthening of skin (bark, etc.) has often preceded a hard winter. Since a warm, wet summer does spurt tree growth and expedite sap flow, a resultant thicker skin might well come before a swing of the pendulum of weather averages, and a cold dryness would then be in order.

When apple blossoms bloom at night
For fifteen days no rain in sight.   **F**

•

APRIL

When April blows her horn [thunder]
It's good for hay and corn.   **P**

If it thunders on All Fool's Day [April 1st]
This assures your crop of hay.   **F**

The colder the April, the better the farm crops.   **F**

•

BEES

A bee was never caught in a shower.   **P**

Bees will not swarm before a storm.   **P**

When bees stay close to the hive, rain is close by.   **T**

All these bee sayings are from observation, and the bee-keeper is always a good weather prophet. He will tell you that "*a swarm of bees in July, does little more than bring a dry.*"

•

BIBLE

"*When ye see a cloud rise out of the west, straightway ye say: There cometh a shower: and so it is.*"—Luke, XII:54.   **T**

In the north temperate zone, where most weather patterns move from west to east, a storm cloud in the west (or a western quadrant) will place you directly in the path of the storm.

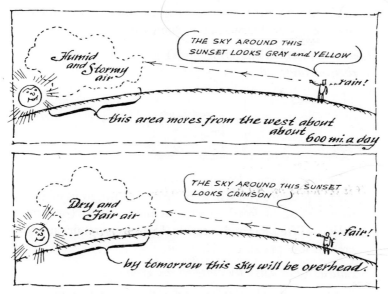

"*When it is evening, ye say, It will be fair weather: for the sky is red. And in the morning, It will be foul weather today: for the sky is red and lowering.*"—Matthew, XVI: 2–3. **T**

Christ, in so speaking, knew that we see the setting sun through air that will reach us tomorrow, as pressure patterns of atmosphere move from west to east. If the setting sun shines through dry air, the sky is reddest; if it shines through moist air, the sky is grayish or yellowish. (These rules apply to the surrounding sky and not the actual disc of the sun.)

BIRDS

South or north, sally forth;
West or east, travel least. **T**

Here is an old saying regarding the migration of geese, which bird watchers say is true. It means that when a flock of geese (on migration flight) flies in a true northerly or southerly direction, the morrow will bring clear weather. But when the flock varies its flight to the west or the east, the morrow will bring rain or snow.

Geese (and other migrating birds) fly higher in fair weather than in foul. **T**

 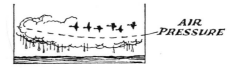

Because pressure lowers as you ascend, the higher you go, the less pressure you will find. Birds seek height in migration to make use of lofty winds, but their ceiling (or altitude limit) is lifted in good-weather, high-pressure air, and lowered in low-pressure, stormy air.

Swallows (and bats) fly close to the ground before a rain. **T**

This is often true, because swallows and bats have very sensitive ear mechanisms, which are affected by sudden changes of air pressure. When there is a sudden drop in atmospheric pressure, they will skim the surface to get as close to the earth as they can and thereby get as high an air pressure as there is at that time.

Sea gull, sea gull, sit on the sand;
It's sign of a rain when you are at hand. **T**

Generally speaking, birds will roost more during low pressure than during high pressure. Before a hurricane great flocks of birds will be seen roosting. Perhaps the lowering pressure or thinning of air density makes flying so much harder; the lessening of natural updrafts would also account for the birds "resting it out."

216

Buds

Look for a heavy winter when the buds have heavy coats. **P**

This saying from Maine might be truest in that section.

•

Candlemas

This day, celebrated on February 2nd, usually heralds the coldest weather in America. Because of this, it became a great weather-forecasting date, when the farmer looked to the sky and hoped to predict what the worst weather of the year would bring. There is no truth in any of the Candlemas sayings, but Candlemas rhymes have lasted throughout the years, as, for example:

If Candlemas be fair and clear,
Two winters will you have this year. **F**

Because the European winter is often over by this date, while in America the coldest days are yet to come, the early pioneers called the American February a "second winter." The idea of a second winter is also hinted at in this old rhyme:

Half the wood and half the hay
You should have on Candlemas Day. **T**

Very true, for a farmer's winter store should be about half used at this date, and the other half can fortify him for the rest of the bad weather.

•

Cattle

When cattle lie down as they are put to pasture, rain is on its way. **F**

A cow with its tail to the west, makes weather the best;
A cow with its tail to the east, makes weather the least. **T**

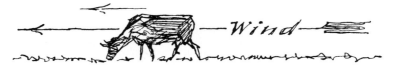

This New England saying has much truth in it, for an animal grazes with its tail to the wind. This is a natural instinct, so the animal may face and see an invader; an invader from the opposite side would carry its scent to the cow, in the wind. Inasmuch as an east wind is a rain wind and a west wind is a fair wind, the grazing animal's tail becomes a weather sign.

•

CHRISTMAS

The twelve days after Christmas indicate the kind of weather for the whole year. Each day in that order indicates the trend of weather for each month in regular order for the following year. **F**

The nearer to a new moon on Christmas, the harder will be the rest of the winter. **F**

Green Christmas, white Easter. **F**

A green Christmas makes a fat churchyard. **F**

The assumption here is that people might take off their "longies" when they dress for the Christmas celebration, and catch cold. The greatest number of pneumonia cases were noticed during the two weeks after Christmas whenever the weather was warm at that time.

CLOUDS

The higher the clouds, the better the weather. **T**

Higher clouds indicate both dryness of air and higher atmospheric pressure. Both these qualities are present with fair weather.

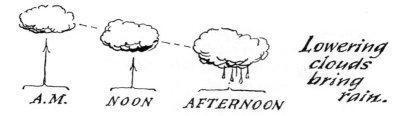

A.M.   NOON   AFTERNOON   *Lowering clouds bring rain.*

Clouds moving in opposite directions indicate rain in about twelve hours. **P**

Cumulus clouds smaller at sunset than at noon, a sign of continued fair weather. **T**

No matter what the ground wind, if high clouds are moving from a westerly quadrant, fair weather will persist. **P**

Wind and wet,   calm and dry

If cirrus mares' tails have ascending streaks or point upward, wind and storm are in the making; if they point downward, calm and dryness are in store. **P**

•

CORN

If corn husks are thicker than usual, a cold winter is ahead. **P**

The Pennsylvanians said, "When the corn wears a heavy coat, so must you." A thicker corn husk is the result of a wetter, warmer summer; a swing of the pendulum to a colder, dryer winter would seem in order in this case.

•

DEW

When the dew is on the grass,
Rain will never come to pass.
When grass is dry at morning light,
Look for rain before the night. **T**

A heavy dew in the evening is the best promise of a dry morrow. Dry grass at night or at sunrise indicates rain before the next noon. This saying is the same as that of England, "*Morn dry, rain nigh; Morn wet, no rain yet.*"

•

DOG

Dog days are when dogs go mad. **F**

The Dog Days are that period when Sirius the Dog Star commands the heavens, rising in conjunction with the sun. Starting about July the 26th, this warm summer period lasts about five weeks. As drought time was often plague time too, many people got the superstitious idea that sickness came with the Dog Star, along with madness.

When a dog eats grass, it is a sign of rain. **P**

You might be surprised that the author finds this saying "possible." His reason is that *an old dog* with rheumatism will find that pre-storm lowering pressure and increased humidity increases his physical discomfort to the amount of an over-all feeling of sickness and pain. The only thing an animal can do in sickness is to purge his system by inducing vomiting; hence the eating of grass.

•

EASTER

Before Easter, winter is not to be trusted. **F**

•

220

FEBRUARY

Thunder in February frightens the maple syrup back into the ground. **P**

This is a New England jingle with truth to it. Not that the sap is really frightened, but sap flow in the maple tree is a very sensitive phenomenon, and unseasonably warm weather (enough to cause heat updraft and thunderclouds) might well cause sap flow to slacken. Maple-sap flow depends upon freezing during the night and thawing during the day.

•

FISH

Near the surface, quick to bite,
Catch your fish when rain's in sight. **P**

Fish in both fresh and salt water tend to sport and bite more eagerly before a rain than directly after one.

When the wind is in the north,
The skillful fisher goes not forth;
When the wind is in the south,
It blows the fly in the fish's mouth. **P**

These lines should have meaning, for they were written by that eminent fisherman, Izaak Walton.

•

FLIES

Flies bite more before a rain. **T**

This rule does not always apply, but insects do cling more during moist weather, as flying is more difficult. Heat causes human sweating, which makes you a more appetizing target. These two reasons, plus a release of more body odors when the atmospheric pressure on your body lowers, will all add

up to the rule that flies and insects are more bothersome just
before a rain than at any other time.

•

FOG

Fog from seaward, weather fair;
Fog from land brings rainy air.   **P**

Much fog in the autumn,
Much snow in the winter.   **P**

These two are from Massachusetts; they are usually true
in that state, but there seems to be no reason to classify them
as general weather truth.

Fog in the morning, sailor take warning;
Fog in the night, sailor's delight.   **P**

There are too many reasons for fog for this saying to be
classed completely true. For example, it is generally accepted
that *"a summer fog for fair and a winter fog for rain."*

Three foggy mornings will bring a rain three times harder
than usual.   **P**

This one from a New Jersey almanac; three foggy mornings in a row, it reasons, would need that much stronger a
rain to purge such static atmosphere.

•

FRIDAY

If the sun sets clear on Friday, it will storm on Sunday.   **F**

The first Friday of each month is an almanac index for the
trend of weather the rest of the month.   **F**

These two sayings from New York State are silly sayings,
but they are still fun to observe.

•

FROGS

When you hear the first frogs in the spring, the frost is out of the ground.   **P**

Generally this is true, yet it also depends upon location and altitude.

•

GRASS

Cobwebs on the grass are a sign of frost.   **T**

Not always, of course, but the "cobwebby grass season" is during late Indian summer, which usually occurs after the first frost and before the second frost.

•

GROUND-HOG DAY

Originally called Candlemas Day (February 2nd).

On this day, in Europe, the bear and badger were supposed to come out to see their shadow. If the animal sees his shadow, this is supposed to frighten him back for another six weeks, and cold weather will last that long. In America the saying refers just to the ground-hog (woodchuck).   **F**

•

GROUSE

When the grouse drums at night, a big snow will fall in the early morning.   **F**

This is an American Indian saying.

•

HAIR

When human hair becomes limp, rain is near.   **T**

There is an American Indian saying that "when locks turn damp in the scalp house, it will rain on the morrow." Hair (particularly blond hair) is still used in hygrometers for measuring humidity.

HALO

Sun or moon halos indicate a coming rain (or snow): the larger the halo, the nearer the precipitation. **T**

This is more likely to be true during warm weather than during midwinter. You are seeing the sun (or moon) through the high ice crystals of cirriform clouds. When these cover the whole sky, it is the sign of an approaching warm front when a long, slow rain will occur. The American Indian puts it thus:

When the sun retires to his house [halo], it is because it is going to rain outside. **T**

The advent of a moon halo after a pale sunset is a fairly certain rain sign. Dr. Edward Jenner said:

"Last night the sun went pale to bed
The moon in halos hid her head." **T**

HURRICANE

June, too soon;
July, stand by;
August, look out!
September you will remember.
October, all over. **T**

This names the hurricane months in America.

Face a hurricane wind and point to your right; you will point to the storm center as it moves along. **T**

This is true of all low-pressure storms, but it is most useful in watching the progress and plotting the exact direction of a hurricane's eye.

•

INDIAN SUMMER

If we don't get a good Indian summer in October or November, we will get it during winter. **F**

Truly American folklore, *Indian summer* is a vague term because no one is completely certain as to its exact date, its origin, or even what the term implies. Generally speaking, it is an unseasonable spell of hot, dry weather that occurs in October. Europe has its counterpart in *"Saint Luke's little summer,"* which begins on the eighteenth of October and ends on the twenty-eighth. The day (October 28th) is supposed to be a day of rain. In America Indian summer was first noted as "a period of late summer heat that occurs right after the first frost." As for the name, some say it originated from its peculiar haze, which resembled "the smoke of Indian fires in the hills." Another explanation is that this was the period when the Indians started out on their fall hunting trips.

•

INSECTS

When the katydid says "Kate," he announces ten days till a frost. **P**

Kate-ee-did-n't . . . 87°
Kate-ee-did . . . . 72°
Kate-ee . . . . . . 65° Summer night temperature
Kate . . . . 58° (°F)
. . . . 55°
mute below 55°F.

225

Coldness numbs all insects and first slackens their calls. When "kate-ee-did!" is reduced to a single "Kate!" it is because of the lowering temperature. The first frost might well be near.

Crickets are accurate thermometers; they chirp faster when warm and slower when cold. **T**

They are extremely accurate. Count their chirps for fourteen seconds, then add forty, and you have the temperature of wherever the cricket is.

When ladybugs swarm
Expect a warm. **F**

•

JULY

If it rains on July 26th, it will rain for the following two weeks. If it is dry, expect two weeks of dryness. **F**

•

JUNE

Wet June, dry September. **F**

•

KILLING

Kill a beetle and it will rain. **F**

Step on an ant and it will rain. **F**

Kill a snake and turn its belly to the sky for rain. **F**

Kill a snake and its body will move till sundown. **F**

•

LEAVES

When the leaves show their backs, it will rain. **T**

When trees grow, their leaves fall into a pattern according to the prevailing wind. Therefore, when a storm wind

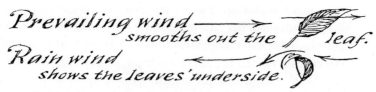

Prevailing wind ———→ smooths out the leaf.
Rain wind ←——— shows the leaves' underside.

(which is naturally a non-prevailing one) occurs, the leaves will be ruffled backwards and show their light undersides.

•

LIGHTNING

Lightning is attracted to mirrors.   **F**

Lightning in the south, brings little else but drought.   **T**

Not drought really, but at least it brings no rain. Because most temperate-zone thunderstorms follow a west-to-east movement, lightning from anywhere except a western quadrant will pass you by without bringing rain.

Yaller gal, yaller gal, flashin' through the night,
Summer storms will pass you by unless the lightnin's white.   **P**

This refers to "heat lightning," which is simply lightning from a storm that is passing you by, or has passed you by, seen far to the south, north, or east. Seen through dusty storm air, it appears red. White lightning is usually that which is seen through clearer air and from a storm which is in a western quadrant and on its way toward you.

Red lightning foretells a dry spell.   **P**

Not a dry spell really, but the storm not reaching you. Explanation of this phenomenon is the same as in the previous saying: you are simply seeing lightning from a storm that is passing by.

Thunder curdles cream.   **F**

Lightning sours milk.   **F**

These two sayings are still believed by most people. Although the old-timers used to cover milk or cream "from lightning," there seems to be no scientific proof that lightning or thunder has any effect on either milk or cream. In the days of no refrigeration, however, the atmospheric effects that caused the storm itself (low pressure, humidity, and heat) would also hasten the spoiling of milk products and make them vulnerable to curdling. So perhaps it was the weather rather than the thunder or lightning!

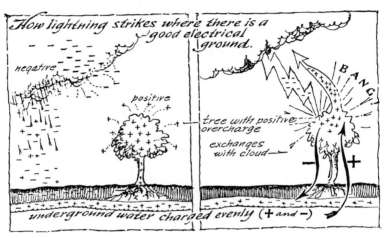

Where lightning strikes, go dig your well. **P**

It has been often true that wherever lightning hit, spring water was close underneath. Lightning is the release of an uneven electrical charge into a more stable reservoir of current. As a vast underground spring cannot change its charge as rapidly as the ground above, a tree whose roots contact a spring makes an excellent target for an exchange of currents and an equalization of potentials.

•

MARCH

In like a lamb, out like a lion;
In like a lion, out like a lamb. **F**

•

MAY

Dry May, wet June. **F**

Cold, wet May,
Barn full of hay. **T**

May 11, 12, and 13 are days of cold weather. **F**

A saying that began in England, where these days were called The Feast of the Three Icemen. The saying persisted here in America after 1816 ("the year without a summer") when a heavy snowstorm during those three days blanketed New England.

•

MILKWEED

Milkweed closes at night before a rainy spell. **P**

The same, however, can be said of the dandelion, clover, and other plants that change their leaf attitude on the approach of rain. The English version is:

Pimpernel, pimpernel, tell me true
Whether the weather be fine or no. **T**

Indeed, the pimpernel closes its petals when the humidity exceeds 80 per cent. Laurel and rhododendron close according to the degrees of coldness.

•

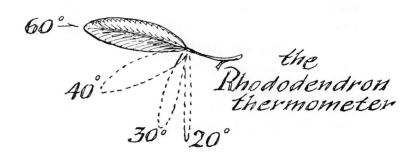

the Rhododendron thermometer

229

MOON

If the moon rises pale, expect rain;
If it rises clear, expect fair.   **P**

Pale moon doth rain,
Red moon doth blow;
White moon doth neither rain nor snow.   **P**

"Pale moon" implies that it is seen through a veil of thin cirriform clouds such as go before a warm air front, which ends in a long, slow rain.

Clear moon, frost soon.   **P**

Moonlit nights have the heaviest frosts.   **T**

Farmers watch for frost during the full moon. Frosts occur when the night is calm and the air clear.

Sharp horns do threaten high winds.   **T**

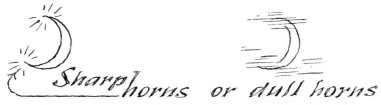

When the crescent moon's ends, or "horns," are clear and sharply defined, it means that high-altitude air is unusually clear as the result of high-speed winds aloft. As winds begin aloft and lower to earth, "sharp horns" on the moon would predict a windy day.

When the moon lies on her back,
She sucks the wet into her lap.   **F**

This from the contention that the moon looks like a dipper that can either hold water or empty it out. With her points turned down, one is supposed to expect rain. There is a similar Tennessee saying:

The crescent moon spills or holds the rain for the coming month. **F**

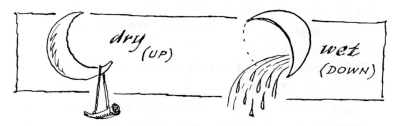

dry (UP)   wet (DOWN)

When you can hang your powder horn on the moon, do just that. **F**

This is a famous Indian saying. What it means is that when the moon's horns are upright enough to "hang something on one," hang up your powder horn, and don't try stalking game, because the woods will be dry for want of rain. Indians did most of their hunting when the ground was wet.

Sir John Herschel devised a table for predicting weather by observing the moon. **P**

This table, credited to Herschel (although he did not claim responsibility), was used in America with great faith. The Pennsylvanian Germans made ornamental "fractur writing" copies of it. For what it is worth, here it is:

First consult your almanac, and observe the following:

If the new moon, first quarter, full moon, or last quarter in summer occurs between

12 and 2 A.M.	*fair*
2 and 4 A.M.	*cold and showers*
4 and 6 A.M.	*rain*
6 and 8 A.M.	*wind and rain*
8 and 10 A.M.	*changeable*
10 and noon	*frequent showers*
12 and 2 P.M.	*much rain*

2 and 4 P.M.	. . . . . .	*changeable*
4 and 6 P.M.	. . . . . .	*fair*
6 and 8 P.M.	. . . . . .	*fair (if wind northwest)*
8 and 10 P.M.	. . . . . .	*rain (if wind south or southwest)*
10 to 12 midnight	. . . . . .	*fair*

If the new moon, first quarter, full moon, or last quarter in winter occurs between

12 and 2 A.M.	. . . . . .	*frost unless wind is southwest*
2 and 4 A.M.	. . . . . .	*snow and wind*
4 and 6 A.M.	. . . . . .	*rain*
6 and 8 A.M.	. . . . . .	*stormy*
8 and 10 A.M.	. . . . . .	*cold if wind westerly*
10 and noon	. . . . . .	*cold and high winds*
12 and 2 P.M.	. . . . . .	*snow and rain*
2 and 4 P.M.	. . . . . .	*fair and mild*
4 and 6 P.M.	. . . . . .	*fair*
6 and 8 P.M.	. . . . . .	*fair and frosty if wind is north*
8 and 10 P.M.	. . . . . .	*rain and snow if wind is south*
10 to 12 midnight	. . . . . .	*fair and frosty*

The moon loses its outline ten hours before rain.   **P**

Not infallible, but often true. The coming of a warm-front ceiling first renders the moon like a ground disc (rain about thirteen hours away); then it loses its shape completely (rain about ten hours away).

•

Moss

Moss dry, sunny sky;
Moss wet, rain you'll get.   **T**

This is a southern-mountain saying. Moss (like human hair) is an excellent material for absorbing atmospheric moisture. In Maine the same saying goes for seaweed.

•

232

NIGHT

When the night has a fever, it cries in the morning. **T**

Although this is an old Indian saying, it probably refers to the meteorological truth that if the temperature increases between 9 P.M. and midnight, rain follows.

•

NORTHERN LIGHTS

Northern lights bring cold weather with them. **P**

This one, the scientists will argue with this author about; for although he can find nothing to back him up on it, he has found cold waves and an aurora over the northern horizon very often occurring at the same time. His contention is that an extremely strong cold wave will carry Arctic particles of auroral quality with it. Although the particles are much higher than the mass of cold air, there is still a long-range magnetic field present. During the past five consecutive auroras (seen as far south as Connecticut) there was a very strong flow of Arctic air present.

•

OCTOBER

Full moon in October without a frost,
No frost till full moon in November. **F**

October has twenty-one fair days. **P**

Indian summer probably prompted this one.

•

ONIONS

Onion skins very thin,
Mild winter coming in;
Onion skins very tough,
Winter's going to be very rough. **P**

This Midwest saying has become almost as popular as the one about the woolly bear. Another Pennsylvania-Dutch version is from Baer's *Agricultural Almanack*; it goes this way:

On New Year's Day scoop out half an onion, one for each month, and place salt therein. After twelve days, the onions in which the salt has dissolved will be the wet months to come. **F**

•

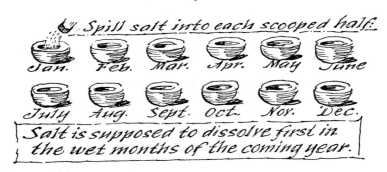

Spill salt into each scooped half:

Jan. Feb. Mar. Apr. May June

July Aug. Sept. Oct. Nov. Dec.

Salt is supposed to dissolve first in the wet months of the coming year.

PONDS

Ponds often turn over during a storm. **P**

Inasmuch as the bottoms of ponds often rise to the top during a heavy downpour, country people call this phenomenon a "turning over." A cold rain falling into a warm pond will settle to the bottom while the warm lower layer will rise to the top. During late summer this "turning over" illusion is most pronounced.

Some storms cause tides in fresh-water lakes. **T**

The effect is like a tide, but the actual cause is the wind. If a lake running east and west is battered by a strong west wind, the body of water piles up at the east end in the form of a high tide.

•

R

The chill is on from near and far
In all the months that have an R. **T**

This was an early-American saying that ended up in restaurant-menu lore regarding the eating of oysters. "One should eat oysters," the saying went, "only during months that contain the letter *R*." Or, as the restaurants put it on their signs, "Oysters *R* in season." The explanation is that all other months have sufficiently warm weather to make oysters liable to have large amounts of dangerous sewage germs in them. Cold water descends and lifts debris to the top.

•

RAIN

Morning rain is like the old lady's dance;
It doesn't last very long.   **P**

This one is from Maine. They also say of this same weather phenomenon:

If the rain waits till noon to visit, prepare for a long visit.   **P**

This means that when you have a threatening morning but the rain doesn't appear till after noon, it will continue into the night and morrow.

Rain long foretold, long last;
Short notice, soon past.   **T**

This one is generally true, because the warm-front rain flows overhead for about ten hours before its tail brushes the ground with rain, and then the warm-air-mass rain lasts for a day or so. The cold-front rain, however, is unannounced, and although it falls harder as a rule, it is soon over.

•

RAINBOW

Rainbow in the morning,
Shepherd take warning;
Rainbow toward night,
Shepherd's delight.   **T**

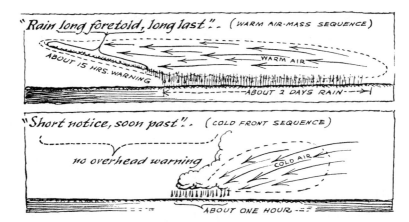

"Rain long foretold, long last". (WARM AIR-MASS SEQUENCE)

ABOUT 15 HRS. WARNING

WARM AIR

ABOUT 2 DAYS RAIN

"Short notice, soon past". (COLD FRONT SEQUENCE)

no overhead warning

COLD AIR

ABOUT ONE HOUR

The modern version of this verse substitutes *sailor* for *shepherd*. Because storm centers usually move from the west, a morning rainbow would have to be seen from a storm already in the west with the eastern sun shining on it. That storm would reach you. But an evening rainbow is seen in the west amid a storm that has already passed you. Therefore, a "shepherd's delight."

It is bad luck to point at a rainbow.   **F**

This is a New York State saying, taken from the Indians. If you point at a rainbow, so the story goes, and the storm god disapproves of you, the rainbow will disappear, but so will you!

•

ROOSTER

When the rooster crows at night,
He tells you that a rain's in sight.   **F**

If the cock crows going to bed,
He wakens with a watery head.   **F**

Cockcrow before two in the morning
Of two days wet it is a warning.   **F**

Some say that a sudden drop of atmospheric pressure or an increase in humidity will waken a rooster into crowing.

•

SAINT SWITHIN'S DAY

If it rains on St. Swithin's Day (July 15th), it will rain for forty days. **F**

From *Poor Robin's Almanack* in 1697, this had been an English saying observed in America too. St. Swithin (the Bishop of Winchester) had a great reverence for rain and asked that he be buried outside the church wall "so that the rain might falleth" upon his grave. This was done, but in the year 971 on July 15th, his body was removed to a tomb within the church, whereupon a great storm broke and lasted for forty days.

•

SAP

When the wind is in the east,
Then the sap will run the least;
When the wind is from the west,
Then the sap will run the best. **T**

From Vermont, this is part of maple-syrup lore. Sap flows when the nights are freezing but the days are thawing. Such a phenomenon occurs almost always during a west wind in New England.

•

SHEEP

When the sheep collect and huddle,
Tomorrow will become a puddle. **P**

This is a western saying, an adaptation of the Indians':

When the buffalo band together, the storm god is herding them. **P**

•

237

SIGHT

The farther the sight, the nearer the rain. **T**

Particularly near the sea, when distant spots loom and appear closer, it is not a sign of clear weather, as many think, but a sign of rain. Haze over the marine horizon during a hot day shows a good degree of evaporation and weather stability. The mixing of air by instability and the lack of evaporation produces clearer air, greater vision, and promise of rain on the morrow.

•

SKY

Evening red and morning gray
Sets the traveler on his way;
Evening gray and morning red
Brings down rain upon his head. **T**

Enough blue sky for a Dutchman's breeches gives the storm just half an hour. **T**

If you can see blue sky during rainfall, you are seeing it through scud clouds in the rear of a low-pressure area.

Mackerel skies and mare's-tails
Make ships carry low sails. **F**

Mare's-tail cirrus can be a fair-weather sign if they are few and scattered. Only a skyful of either cirrus or mackerel (cirro-cumulus that resembles rippled sand) can mean that a storm is approaching.

•

238

SMELL

When ditches and cellars smell most, a long rain is near.   **T**

As the weight of high-pressure (fair-weather) atmosphere keeps a certain amount of the odors trapped, a lessening of

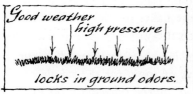
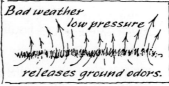

pressure (as before a storm) will release odors from walls, swamps, ditches, cellars, etc. One almanac put it:

When the ditch offends the nose,
Look for rain and stormy blows.

•

SMOKE

When smoke descends, good weather ends.   **T**

The instability of pre-storm pressures and humidity keeps smoke from chimneys or bonfires from rising quickly, finally to curl downward in the face of a storm wind.

•

SNAKE

Bury a snake, good weather to make,
Hanging it high brings storm clouds nigh.   **F**

Because snakes often writhe for a long time after death, the legend is that "a snake will move till sundown." Many other superstitions also involve dead snakes. Country people often bury a dead snake "to keep rain away," but it is possible that the original reason was really just to keep away the smell.

•

Snow

If the first snowflakes of a snowstorm are large, this means the storm will last; smallish first flakes indicate a short storm. **P**

Although this is not always true, large flakes are merely masses of smaller flakes stuck together, and the turbulence and wetness that caused the flakes to stick both result in a storm condition of lasting variety.

The day of the month on which the first snowfall occurs indicates the number of days of snow for the whole coming winter. If the first snow falls on the thirteenth, for example, there will be thirteen snowstorms during the coming winter. **F**

On a stove melt a pint of snow from the first snowfall; the number of bubbles rising to the surface will tell you the number of snowfalls for the season. **F**

If snow commences near noon, it shall be heavy.

Or as the almanac said:

If snow begins in mid of day,
Expect a foot of it to lay. **P**

You can't generalize on this one, but because heavy precipitation is often the result of a strong cold wave and this wave moves in upon the warmer air of midday, the resulting storm is liable to be a strong one.

•

Soap

When drops collect on soap,
For rainfall you can hope. **P**

Not so much with modern soap, but when people made their own soap, humidity in the atmosphere collected rapidly on the surface of a cake of soap, particularly after a long dry spell.

•

Soot

When soot falls down the chimney, rain is near. **P**

The theory is that delicate soot is held in place by air's heavy pressure and dryness, along with some atmospheric magnetism. Therefore when air pressure lowers and dampness enters the picture, electric atmospheric phenomena lessens too, and the soot is loosened.

•

Sound

Sound traveling far and wide
A stormy day this does betide. **T**

This verse from old English farm books is a saying with merit, for you actually can "hear bad weather approaching," according to country people. Faraway sounds such as train whistles, droning airplanes, or distant birdcalls sound hollow or as if heard down a long corridor, and predict a long siege of rain, such as a warm-front storm.

•

Spiders

When spiders forsake their webs one day, look for rain the next. **F**

Spiders spin webs on the grass during Indian summer. **T**

As told in Eric Sloane's *Look at the Sky*, the tiny gossamer spider is known for its webs that appear on the grass as dewy strands during Indian-summer mornings. In fact the word *gossamer* comes from "goose summer," or the early-English name for our Indian summer period.

•

Squirrels

When squirrels lay in a big store of nuts, look for a hard winter. **F**

Squirrels just do the best they can, and some years have better nut seasons than others. Yet the old-timers still observe the activities of the squirrels as a sign of winter weather.

•

STARS

The Dog Star brings drought.   **P**

Not that the star itself causes drought, but when the **Dog Star**, Sirius, is most evident, droughts are most liable to occur, because of the lack of rainfall at that season.

When the stars begin to hide
Soon the rain it will betide.   **T**

Increasing humidity and haze precede a spell of rain and cause the stars to fade.

•

SUN

The sun "drawing water" indicates the coming of rain.   **F**

"Sky rays" are no weather sign

The sun cannot "draw water" here as *these* rays are shadow or lack of sunshine.

The sunlight always draws water by means of evaporation. Usually where we see shafts of light and shadow, the sun is *not* drawing water. Because there must be less evap-

242

oration in the presence of shadow, when you see such shafts of dark with sunlight between, you might say, "See—there the sun is *not* drawing water."

When the sun sets unhappy [with a veiled face], the morning will be angry with storm.—Zuni Indians **T**

Because weather usually moves from west to east, you see the setting sun through atmosphere that will reach you later on; when that "atmosphere to come" is moist and veiled by high cirrus clouds, you will find rain commanding the morning.

A sunshiny shower
Won't last out the hour. **T**

If the rain clouds are so scattered and confined as to admit sunshine between them, the cloud cover is indeed breaking up, and the storm is about to cease.

•

SUNDAY

If it storms the first Sunday of the month, it will storm every Sunday of the month. **F**

This is an old circus saying, also applying to "the first Saturday of the month." Silly as it seems, records have been kept showing it to be as much as 90 per cent true over a period of ten years, according to circus people.

•

SWINE

Hogs should be slaughtered after the second frost, in the dark of the moon. **P**

Country slaughtering is always done after the warm spell that follows the first frost, assuring coolness to keep the hanging meat from spoiling. The "dark of the moon," however, probably referred to the superstition that moon rays spoil meat, which is untrue. The first Department of

Agriculture *Weather Book* said that "moonbeams produce certain chemical results that spoil fish and some kinds of meat." This superstition was printed by that organization as late as 1903.

•

TELEPHONE WIRES

Telephone wires [or telegraph wires] hum and whine when a weather change is due. **T**

When cold, dry air arrives, wires tighten and cause a high-pitched humming sound. With the arrival of cold air a short storm usually occurs at the onset of the air mass. This singing of wires is loudest in winter.

•

THUNDER

Thunder at morn,
Wind is born;
Thunder at noon,
Rain comes soon;
Thunder at eve,
A tempest will weave. **F**

Thunder in spring,
Cold will bring. **F**

Thunder is of almost no value in the prediction of storm paths, except that thunder from a western quadrant is from a storm that is most certain to reach you.

•

TREES

Trees grow dark before a storm. **T**

Generally speaking, the landscape reflects the sky, either by water or by the glossiness of a solid tree pattern. This truth, however, is a very subtle phenomenon.

•

TURKEY

If turkey feathers are unusually thick by Thanksgiving, look for a hard winter. **F**

A dark breastbone in a Thanksgiving Day turkey indicates a
hardy winter to come. **F**

•

WATER

When the spring that's low
Begins to flow,
Then sure we know
It will rain or snow. **P**

This is a southern-mountain saying. Generally speaking,
this is not true, but there are many springs and wells that *do*
respond to pre-storm pressures and begin to flow just before
precipitation. This is supposedly caused by the drop in outside atmospheric pressure.

•

WEDDING

A rainy wedding day
Makes the skies of marriage gray. **F**

An old hillbilly saying; indeed, weddings have been
called off in Arkansas because of the weather.

•

WILD AZALEA

When the wild azalea shuts its doors,
That's when winter tempest roars. **P**

•

WIND

When the wind is in the east
'Tis neither good for man nor beast. **P**

This is most true along the Atlantic coast where an east wind blows wetness into the land areas, while it presages a warm air-mass storm from the south (which usually brings a long-lasting type of rainfall).

An easterly wind is like a boring guest that hasn't sense enough to leave. **P**

In many coastal areas, the storm with easterly winds proves the most long-lasting. It frequently shifts between northeast and east for two days.

High-altitude winds soon descend to earth. **T**

Winds do tend to originate aloft and settle to earth. By observing the direction of high-altitude clouds, you may tell what the wind direction at earth level will be in a few hours or the following day. This effect explains the following New Hampshire saying:

The storm alights on the mountain, and walks into the valley before the rain arrives. **T**

The east wind brings aches and pains. **P**

Humidity plus lowering pressure does seem to affect the nerves, causing old wounds, etc., to begin hurting. The almanac said that

With coming storm your aching corns presage,
And aches will throb, your hollow tooth will rage.

A west wind is a favorable wind. **T**

This is the temperate-zone prevailing wind of favorable weather. It is the wind that follows all storms and is associated with clearing and good spirits. Benjamin Franklin said, "Do business with men when the wind is in the west, when the barometer is high."

A west wind like an honest man, goes to bed at sundown. **P**

246

This favorable wind is lessened by the cooling off of land areas after the sun lowers and sets.

The worst winds are at the end of the storm. **P**

In an ordinary gale the wind often blows hardest when the barometer is just beginning to recover from a low.

North to west, sugar's best;
South to east, flow is least. **T**

Maple-sap flow depends on a sharp freeze at night and a good thaw during day. This happens with a north or west wind and cannot occur with a south or east wind.

Wind direction is the major sign for storm prophesy. The first United States (Department of Agriculture) Weather Book lists the following rules for using wind to predict weather.

1. Westerly winds (southwest to northwest) are fair-weather winds.
2. When during a storm the wind shifts from east to west, clearing follows.
3. Over a great part of the United States a steady and strong south-to-east wind will bring rain within thirty-six hours.
4. Easterly winds bring rain; northeast winds in winter bring heavy snow.

•

Woolly Bear

The amount of brown on the woolly bear (that part in the middle) foretells the severity of the coming winter. **P**

At least many weather experts have been mystified by this one. The wider the middle band, the milder the winter.

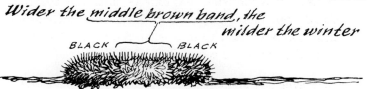

Wider the middle brown band, the milder the winter

BLACK   BLACK

Other books by Eric Sloane
available as Dover reprints

ABC Book of Early Americana
A Museum of Early American Tools
American Barns and Covered Bridges
American Yesterday
A Reverence for Wood
Look at the Sky and Tell the Weather
Our Vanishing Landscape
Diary of an Early American Boy: Noah Blake 1805
The Seasons of America Past
The Cracker Barrel
Once Upon a Time: The Way America Was
Eric Sloane's Weather Book
Recollections in Black and White
*Return to Taos: Eric Sloane's Sketchbook of Roadside
    Americana*
Skies and the Artist: How to Draw Clouds and Sunsets
Eric Sloane's Book of Storms: Hurricanes, Twisters and Squalls
For Spacious Skies: A Sketchbook of American Weather
The Little Red Schoolhouse

(Log on to www.doverpublications.com for more information.)

A CATALOG OF SELECTED
DOVER BOOKS
IN ALL FIELDS OF INTEREST

A CATALOG OF SELECTED DOVER
BOOKS IN ALL FIELDS OF INTEREST

100 BEST-LOVED POEMS, Edited by Philip Smith. "The Passionate Shepherd to His Love," "Shall I compare thee to a summer's day?" "Death, be not proud," "The Raven," "The Road Not Taken," plus works by Blake, Wordsworth, Byron, Shelley, Keats, many others. 96pp. 5³⁄₁₆ x 8¼.   0-486-28553-7

100 SMALL HOUSES OF THE THIRTIES, Brown-Blodgett Company. Exterior photographs and floor plans for 100 charming structures. Illustrations of models accompanied by descriptions of interiors, color schemes, closet space, and other amenities. 200 illustrations. 112pp. 8⅜ x 11.   0-486-44131-8

1000 TURN-OF-THE-CENTURY HOUSES: With Illustrations and Floor Plans, Herbert C. Chivers. Reproduced from a rare edition, this showcase of homes ranges from cottages and bungalows to sprawling mansions. Each house is meticulously illustrated and accompanied by complete floor plans. 256pp. 9⅜ x 12¼.
0-486-45596-3

101 GREAT AMERICAN POEMS, Edited by The American Poetry & Literacy Project. Rich treasury of verse from the 19th and 20th centuries includes works by Edgar Allan Poe, Robert Frost, Walt Whitman, Langston Hughes, Emily Dickinson, T. S. Eliot, other notables. 96pp. 5³⁄₁₆ x 8¼.   0-486-40158-8

101 GREAT SAMURAI PRINTS, Utagawa Kuniyoshi. Kuniyoshi was a master of the warrior woodblock print — and these 18th-century illustrations represent the pinnacle of his craft. Full-color portraits of renowned Japanese samurais pulse with movement, passion, and remarkably fine detail. 112pp. 8⅜ x 11.   0-486-46523-3

ABC OF BALLET, Janet Grosser. Clearly worded, abundantly illustrated little guide defines basic ballet-related terms: arabesque, battement, pas de chat, relevé, sissonne, many others. Pronunciation guide included. Excellent primer. 48pp. 4³⁄₁₆ x 5¾.
0-486-40871-X

ACCESSORIES OF DRESS: An Illustrated Encyclopedia, Katherine Lester and Bess Viola Oerke. Illustrations of hats, veils, wigs, cravats, shawls, shoes, gloves, and other accessories enhance an engaging commentary that reveals the humor and charm of the many-sided story of accessorized apparel. 644 figures and 59 plates. 608pp. 6⅛ x 9¼.
0-486-43378-1

ADVENTURES OF HUCKLEBERRY FINN, Mark Twain. Join Huck and Jim as their boyhood adventures along the Mississippi River lead them into a world of excitement, danger, and self-discovery. Humorous narrative, lyrical descriptions of the Mississippi valley, and memorable characters. 224pp. 5³⁄₁₆ x 8¼.   0-486-28061-6

ALICE STARMORE'S BOOK OF FAIR ISLE KNITTING, Alice Starmore. A noted designer from the region of Scotland's Fair Isle explores the history and techniques of this distinctive, stranded-color knitting style and provides copious illustrated instructions for 14 original knitwear designs. 208pp. 8⅜ x 10⅞.   0-486-47218-3

Browse over 9,000 books at www.doverpublications.com

ALICE'S ADVENTURES IN WONDERLAND, Lewis Carroll. Beloved classic about a little girl lost in a topsy-turvy land and her encounters with the White Rabbit, March Hare, Mad Hatter, Cheshire Cat, and other delightfully improbable characters. 42 illustrations by Sir John Tenniel. 96pp. 5³⁄₁₆ x 8¼.   0-486-27543-4

AMERICA'S LIGHTHOUSES: An Illustrated History, Francis Ross Holland. Profusely illustrated fact-filled survey of American lighthouses since 1716. Over 200 stations — East, Gulf, and West coasts, Great Lakes, Hawaii, Alaska, Puerto Rico, the Virgin Islands, and the Mississippi and St. Lawrence Rivers. 240pp. 8 x 10¾.
       0-486-25576-X

AN ENCYCLOPEDIA OF THE VIOLIN, Alberto Bachmann. Translated by Frederick H. Martens. Introduction by Eugene Ysaye. First published in 1925, this renowned reference remains unsurpassed as a source of essential information, from construction and evolution to repertoire and technique. Includes a glossary and 73 illustrations. 496pp. 6½ x 9¼.   0-486-46618-3

ANIMALS: 1,419 Copyright-Free Illustrations of Mammals, Birds, Fish, Insects, etc., Selected by Jim Harter. Selected for its visual impact and ease of use, this outstanding collection of wood engravings presents over 1,000 species of animals in extremely lifelike poses. Includes mammals, birds, reptiles, amphibians, fish, insects, and other invertebrates. 284pp. 9 x 12.   0-486-23766-4

THE ANNALS, Tacitus. Translated by Alfred John Church and William Jackson Brodribb. This vital chronicle of Imperial Rome, written by the era's great historian, spans A.D. 14-68 and paints incisive psychological portraits of major figures, from Tiberius to Nero. 416pp. 5³⁄₁₆ x 8¼.   0-486-45236-0

ANTIGONE, Sophocles. Filled with passionate speeches and sensitive probing of moral and philosophical issues, this powerful and often-performed Greek drama reveals the grim fate that befalls the children of Oedipus. Footnotes. 64pp. 5³⁄₁₆ x 8 ¼.   0-486-27804-2

ART DECO DECORATIVE PATTERNS IN FULL COLOR, Christian Stoll. Reprinted from a rare 1910 portfolio, 160 sensuous and exotic images depict a breathtaking array of florals, geometrics, and abstracts — all elegant in their stark simplicity. 64pp. 8⅜ x 11.   0-486-44862-2

THE ARTHUR RACKHAM TREASURY: 86 Full-Color Illustrations, Arthur Rackham. Selected and Edited by Jeff A. Menges. A stunning treasury of 86 full-page plates span the famed English artist's career, from *Rip Van Winkle* (1905) to masterworks such as *Undine, A Midsummer Night's Dream,* and *Wind in the Willows* (1939). 96pp. 8⅜ x 11.
       0-486-44685-9

THE AUTHENTIC GILBERT & SULLIVAN SONGBOOK, W. S. Gilbert and A. S. Sullivan. The most comprehensive collection available, this songbook includes selections from every one of Gilbert and Sullivan's light operas. Ninety-two numbers are presented uncut and unedited, and in their original keys. 410pp. 9 x 12.
       0-486-23482-7

THE AWAKENING, Kate Chopin. First published in 1899, this controversial novel of a New Orleans wife's search for love outside a stifling marriage shocked readers. Today, it remains a first-rate narrative with superb characterization. New introductory Note. 128pp. 5³⁄₁₆ x 8¼.   0-486-27786-0

BASIC DRAWING, Louis Priscilla. Beginning with perspective, this commonsense manual progresses to the figure in movement, light and shade, anatomy, drapery, composition, trees and landscape, and outdoor sketching. Black-and-white illustrations throughout. 128pp. 8⅜ x 11.   0-486-45815-6

Browse over 9,000 books at www.doverpublications.com

THE BATTLES THAT CHANGED HISTORY, Fletcher Pratt. Historian profiles 16 crucial conflicts, ancient to modern, that changed the course of Western civilization. Gripping accounts of battles led by Alexander the Great, Joan of Arc, Ulysses S. Grant, other commanders. 27 maps. 352pp. 5⅜ x 8½. 0-486-41129-X

BEETHOVEN'S LETTERS, Ludwig van Beethoven. Edited by Dr. A. C. Kalischer. Features 457 letters to fellow musicians, friends, greats, patrons, and literary men. Reveals musical thoughts, quirks of personality, insights, and daily events. Includes 15 plates. 410pp. 5⅜ x 8½. 0-486-22769-3

BERNICE BOBS HER HAIR AND OTHER STORIES, F. Scott Fitzgerald. This brilliant anthology includes 6 of Fitzgerald's most popular stories: "The Diamond as Big as the Ritz," the title tale, "The Offshore Pirate," "The Ice Palace," "The Jelly Bean," and "May Day." 176pp. 5⅜ x 8½. 0-486-47049-0

BESLER'S BOOK OF FLOWERS AND PLANTS: 73 Full-Color Plates from Hortus Eystettensis, 1613, Basilius Besler. Here is a selection of magnificent plates from the *Hortus Eystettensis*, which vividly illustrated and identified the plants, flowers, and trees that thrived in the legendary German garden at Eichstätt. 80pp. 8⅜ x 11. 0-486-46005-3

THE BOOK OF KELLS, Edited by Blanche Cirker. Painstakingly reproduced from a rare facsimile edition, this volume contains full-page decorations, portraits, illustrations, plus a sampling of textual leaves with exquisite calligraphy and ornamentation. 32 full-color illustrations. 32pp. 9⅜ x 12¼. 0-486-24345-1

THE BOOK OF THE CROSSBOW: With an Additional Section on Catapults and Other Siege Engines, Ralph Payne-Gallwey. Fascinating study traces history and use of crossbow as military and sporting weapon, from Middle Ages to modern times. Also covers related weapons: balistas, catapults, Turkish bows, more. Over 240 illustrations. 400pp. 7¼ x 10⅛. 0-486-28720-3

THE BUNGALOW BOOK: Floor Plans and Photos of 112 Houses, 1910, Henry L. Wilson. Here are 112 of the most popular and economic blueprints of the early 20th century — plus an illustration or photograph of each completed house. A wonderful time capsule that still offers a wealth of valuable insights. 160pp. 8⅜ x 11. 0-486-45104-6

THE CALL OF THE WILD, Jack London. A classic novel of adventure, drawn from London's own experiences as a Klondike adventurer, relating the story of a heroic dog caught in the brutal life of the Alaska Gold Rush. Note. 64pp. 5³⁄₁₆ x 8¼. 0-486-26472-6

CANDIDE, Voltaire. Edited by Francois-Marie Arouet. One of the world's great satires since its first publication in 1759. Witty, caustic skewering of romance, science, philosophy, religion, government — nearly all human ideals and institutions. 112pp. 5³⁄₁₆ x 8¼. 0-486-26689-3

CELEBRATED IN THEIR TIME: Photographic Portraits from the George Grantham Bain Collection, Edited by Amy Pastan. With an Introduction by Michael Carlebach. Remarkable portrait gallery features 112 rare images of Albert Einstein, Charlie Chaplin, the Wright Brothers, Henry Ford, and other luminaries from the worlds of politics, art, entertainment, and industry. 128pp. 8⅜ x 11. 0-486-46754-6

CHARIOTS FOR APOLLO: The NASA History of Manned Lunar Spacecraft to 1969, Courtney G. Brooks, James M. Grimwood, and Loyd S. Swenson, Jr. This illustrated history by a trio of experts is the definitive reference on the Apollo spacecraft and lunar modules. It traces the vehicles' design, development, and operation in space. More than 100 photographs and illustrations. 576pp. 6¾ x 9¼. 0-486-46756-2

Browse over 9,000 books at www.doverpublications.com

A CHRISTMAS CAROL, Charles Dickens. This engrossing tale relates Ebenezer Scrooge's ghostly journeys through Christmases past, present, and future and his ultimate transformation from a harsh and grasping old miser to a charitable and compassionate human being. 80pp. 5³⁄₁₆ x 8¼.   0-486-26865-9

COMMON SENSE, Thomas Paine. First published in January of 1776, this highly influential landmark document clearly and persuasively argued for American separation from Great Britain and paved the way for the Declaration of Independence. 64pp. 5³⁄₁₆ x 8¼.   0-486-29602-4

THE COMPLETE SHORT STORIES OF OSCAR WILDE, Oscar Wilde. Complete texts of "The Happy Prince and Other Tales," "A House of Pomegranates," "Lord Arthur Savile's Crime and Other Stories," "Poems in Prose," and "The Portrait of Mr. W. H." 208pp. 5³⁄₁₆ x 8¼.   0-486-45216-6

COMPLETE SONNETS, William Shakespeare. Over 150 exquisite poems deal with love, friendship, the tyranny of time, beauty's evanescence, death, and other themes in language of remarkable power, precision, and beauty. Glossary of archaic terms. 80pp. 5³⁄₁₆ x 8¼.   0-486-26686-9

THE COUNT OF MONTE CRISTO: Abridged Edition, Alexandre Dumas. Falsely accused of treason, Edmond Dantès is imprisoned in the bleak Chateau d'If. After a hair-raising escape, he launches an elaborate plot to extract a bitter revenge against those who betrayed him. 448pp. 5³⁄₁₆ x 8¼.   0-486-45643-9

CRAFTSMAN BUNGALOWS: Designs from the Pacific Northwest, Yoho & Merritt. This reprint of a rare catalog, showcasing the charming simplicity and cozy style of Craftsman bungalows, is filled with photos of completed homes, plus floor plans and estimated costs. An indispensable resource for architects, historians, and illustrators. 112pp. 10 x 7.   0-486-46875-5

CRAFTSMAN BUNGALOWS: 59 Homes from "The Craftsman," Edited by Gustav Stickley. Best and most attractive designs from Arts and Crafts Movement publication — 1903–1916 — includes sketches, photographs of homes, floor plans, descriptive text. 128pp. 8¼ x 11.   0-486-25829-7

CRIME AND PUNISHMENT, Fyodor Dostoyevsky. Translated by Constance Garnett. Supreme masterpiece tells the story of Raskolnikov, a student tormented by his own thoughts after he murders an old woman. Overwhelmed by guilt and terror, he confesses and goes to prison. 480pp. 5³⁄₁₆ x 8¼.   0-486-41587-2

THE DECLARATION OF INDEPENDENCE AND OTHER GREAT DOCUMENTS OF AMERICAN HISTORY: 1775-1865, Edited by John Grafton. Thirteen compelling and influential documents: Henry's "Give Me Liberty or Give Me Death," Declaration of Independence, The Constitution, Washington's First Inaugural Address, The Monroe Doctrine, The Emancipation Proclamation, Gettysburg Address, more. 64pp. 5³⁄₁₆ x 8¼.   0-486-41124-9

THE DESERT AND THE SOWN: Travels in Palestine and Syria, Gertrude Bell. "The female Lawrence of Arabia," Gertrude Bell wrote captivating, perceptive accounts of her travels in the Middle East. This intriguing narrative, accompanied by 160 photos, traces her 1905 sojourn in Lebanon, Syria, and Palestine. 368pp. 5⅜ x 8½.   0-486-46876-3

A DOLL'S HOUSE, Henrik Ibsen. Ibsen's best-known play displays his genius for realistic prose drama. An expression of women's rights, the play climaxes when the central character, Nora, rejects a smothering marriage and life in "a doll's house." 80pp. 5³⁄₁₆ x 8¼.   0-486-27062-9

Browse over 9,000 books at www.doverpublications.com

DOOMED SHIPS: Great Ocean Liner Disasters, William H. Miller, Jr. Nearly 200 photographs, many from private collections, highlight tales of some of the vessels whose pleasure cruises ended in catastrophe: the *Morro Castle, Normandie, Andrea Doria, Europa,* and many others. 128pp. 8⅜ x 11¾. 0-486-45366-9

THE DORÉ BIBLE ILLUSTRATIONS, Gustave Doré. Detailed plates from the Bible: the Creation scenes, Adam and Eve, horrifying visions of the Flood, the battle sequences with their monumental crowds, depictions of the life of Jesus, 241 plates in all. 241pp. 9 x 12. 0-486-23004-X

DRAWING DRAPERY FROM HEAD TO TOE, Cliff Young. Expert guidance on how to draw shirts, pants, skirts, gloves, hats, and coats on the human figure, including folds in relation to the body, pull and crush, action folds, creases, more. Over 200 drawings. 48pp. 8¼ x 11. 0-486-45591-2

DUBLINERS, James Joyce. A fine and accessible introduction to the work of one of the 20th century's most influential writers, this collection features 15 tales, including a masterpiece of the short-story genre, "The Dead." 160pp. 5³⁄₁₆ x 8¼. 0-486-26870-5

EASY-TO-MAKE POP-UPS, Joan Irvine. Illustrated by Barbara Reid. Dozens of wonderful ideas for three-dimensional paper fun — from holiday greeting cards with moving parts to a pop-up menagerie. Easy-to-follow, illustrated instructions for more than 30 projects. 299 black-and-white illustrations. 96pp. 8⅜ x 11. 0-486-44622-0

EASY-TO-MAKE STORYBOOK DOLLS: A "Novel" Approach to Cloth Dollmaking, Sherralyn St. Clair. Favorite fictional characters come alive in this unique beginner's dollmaking guide. Includes patterns for Pollyanna, Dorothy from *The Wonderful Wizard of Oz,* Mary of *The Secret Garden,* plus easy-to-follow instructions, 263 black-and-white illustrations, and an 8-page color insert. 112pp. 8¼ x 11. 0-486-47360-0

EINSTEIN'S ESSAYS IN SCIENCE, Albert Einstein. Speeches and essays in accessible, everyday language profile influential physicists such as Niels Bohr and Isaac Newton. They also explore areas of physics to which the author made major contributions. 128pp. 5 x 8. 0-486-47011-3

EL DORADO: Further Adventures of the Scarlet Pimpernel, Baroness Orczy. A popular sequel to *The Scarlet Pimpernel,* this suspenseful story recounts the Pimpernel's attempts to rescue the Dauphin from imprisonment during the French Revolution. An irresistible blend of intrigue, period detail, and vibrant characterizations. 352pp. 5³⁄₁₆ x 8¼. 0-486-44026-5

ELEGANT SMALL HOMES OF THE TWENTIES: 99 Designs from a Competition, Chicago Tribune. Nearly 100 designs for five- and six-room houses feature New England and Southern colonials, Normandy cottages, stately Italianate dwellings, and other fascinating snapshots of American domestic architecture of the 1920s. 112pp. 9 x 12. 0-486-46910-7

THE ELEMENTS OF STYLE: The Original Edition, William Strunk, Jr. This is the book that generations of writers have relied upon for timeless advice on grammar, diction, syntax, and other essentials. In concise terms, it identifies the principal requirements of proper style and common errors. 64pp. 5⅜ x 8½. 0-486-44798-7

THE ELUSIVE PIMPERNEL, Baroness Orczy. Robespierre's revolutionaries find their wicked schemes thwarted by the heroic Pimpernel — Sir Percival Blakeney. In this thrilling sequel, Chauvelin devises a plot to eliminate the Pimpernel and his wife. 272pp. 5³⁄₁₆ x 8¼. 0-486-45464-9

Browse over 9,000 books at www.doverpublications.com